ULSTER SAILS WEST

The Story of the Great Emigration from Ulster to North America in the 18th Century, Together with an Outline of the Part Played by Ulstermen in Building the United States

By
WILLIAM F. MARSHALL

GENEALOGICAL PUBLISHING CO., INC.
Baltimore 1984

This edition first published:
Belfast, Ireland, 1950
Reprinted: Genealogical Publishing Co., Inc.
Baltimore, 1977, 1979, 1984
Reprinted from a volume in the library of the
University of California, Berkeley
Library of Congress Catalogue Card Number 76-56641
International Standard Book Number 0-8063-0754-4
Made in the United States of America

Ulster Sails West

The Story of the Great Emigration from Ulster to North America in the 18th century, together with an outline of the part played by Ulstermen in building the United States.

BY

W. F. MARSHALL.

PRINTED IN IRELAND

FIRST EDITION	..	..	DECEMBER, 1943
SECOND EDITION	..	..	FEBRUARY, 1944
THIRD EDITION	..	..	JUNE, 1950.

Hi! Uncle Sam!
When freedom was denied you,
And Imperial might defied you,
Who was it stood beside you
*   At Quebec and Brandywine?*
And dared retreats and dangers,
Red-coats and Hessian strangers,
In the lean, long-rifled Rangers,
*   And the Pennsylvania Line!*

Hi! Uncle Sam!
Wherever there was fighting,
Or wrong that needed righting,
An Ulsterman was sighting
*   His Kentucky gun with care:*
All the road to Yorktown,
From Lexington to Yorktown,
From Valley Forge to Yorktown,
*   That Ulsterman was there!*

Hi! Uncle Sam!
Virginia sent her brave men,
The North paraded grave men,
That they might not be slave men,
*   But ponder this with calm:*
The first to face the Tory,
And the first to lift Old Glory
Made your war an Ulster story:
*   Think it over, Uncle Sam!*

ULSTER'S MARK ON THE UNITED STATES

O God our help in ages past,
Our hope for years to come;
Be Thou our guard while troubles last,
And our eternal home.

MY purpose in these pages is to tell the story of the part played in the making of the United States by people of Ulster origin and descent. It is a great story. I am embarrassed by the abundance of material for it, and to cover the ground in a booklet I must omit much that is of interest. I am debarred from brightness of detail. The story has to be severely factual, and it is only in outline that I can tell it here.

The story is not so generally known as it should be, even in Ulster. Much publicity has been given to the fact that a large number of United States Presidents have had the Ulster blood, and Press references to great Americans of Ulster stock have not been uncommon. Due credit must also be given to historians who have recorded the emigration of Ulstermen to America in the 18th century, and have examined the general situation which produced it.

But the average man is not a student of history, and such knowledge of it as he may be expected to acquire must come to him in handy and popular form. Hitherto no brief yet comprehensive outline of Ulster's mark on the United States has been available. My hope is that these pages may supply, however imperfectly, what I believe to be an urgent need.

And this need is the more urgent, now that the American flag so often decorates our Ulster countryside, and we have ceased to stare at American soldiers walking in our streets.* Few of these welcome friends have heard our story. For, in America too, the average man is not a student, and the work done by his own historians does not come readily to his hand and eye.

Moreover, in America itself, and far outside it, our story has been overshadowed by the story of the Puritan achievement in New England, and the story of the Cavalier achievement in Virginia. These people had the start of our people in America, and their stories got the start of any other.

But, after all, the story of ' Ulster and America ' has been often confused with that of ' Ireland in America.' It has been frequently acclaimed as the Irish contribution to the making of the United States. To so acclaim it is not unfair, so long as we make clear the part of Ireland the contribution came from. What is most unfair and dishonest is to claim this contribution as Irish, and then use it as the basis of propaganda against the Ulster that made it.

Unhappily this kind of dishonesty has been frequent. But simply to rail against it is vain work. The best antidote to such poison is the truth.

Ulster Sails West

Now to estimate the Ulster achievement it is necessary, first of all, to prove that an achievement was

* 1943.

possible. It is necessary to prove that Ulstermen were in America in sufficient numbers to make possible a great Ulster contribution to the United States. My first task, therefore, is to make it clear that from the year 1718, and all through that century a continuous stream of emigration poured from the North of Ireland, a stream that, at frequent intervals became a roaring flood. This great outflow was almost entirely Protestant, and mainly Presbyterian.

Why?

Some words need to be said here about the causes of this emigration. There was a variety of causes, all of which influenced, more or less, the people concerned.

There was religion. After the siege of Derry, a certain amount of toleration was granted to Presbyterians, out of gratitude for services rendered by them during the war. But there were still grievances that were unredressed. The validity of Presbyterian marriages was denied.[1] Dissenters were barred from teaching in schools. They were compelled to serve as church-wardens. They were often not allowed to bury their dead without the funeral service of the Established Church. Moreover, in the reign of Queen Anne, the Sacramental Test for all office-holders was restored, and there was considerable interference with Presbyterian ministers and Presbyterian worship.[2] This curtailment of toleration roused much resentment, and many Presbyterians regarded it as black ingratitude. They recalled that without their services

Derry could not have been held, and King William would have been left without a bridge-head in Ireland. On the other hand, Archbishop Boulter contended that religious intolerance was not a factor leading to the emigration, and that the blame for it was chiefly due to high rents;[3] while the Irish gentry on a Commons' Committee reported that "the inclination to emigrate is increased by the new and burdensome demand made by the clergy of the tithe of agistment."[4] If we accept the Archbishop's view, we must disbelieve what the early emigrants said after their arrival in America[5]—and presumably they should have known the reasons that induced them to go— and we must also dispute the verdict of the most eminent historians on both sides of the ocean.

It is not, however, contended here that religious intolerance was the only factor or even the only important factor leading to this emigration. There were six years of drought between 1714 and 1719.[6] There was disease that caused a high death-rate in sheep in 1716.[7] There was an outbreak of small-pox in 1718.[8] There was a scarcity of silver and copper coin that hampered trade.[9] The woollen industry had languished, and the linen trade was not flourishing.[10] There were three very bad harvests in 1725, 1726, and 1727, so that in 1728 the price of food was higher than in living memory,[11] and the minister of Templepatrick declared that there was not seed enough to sow the ground.[12] There was a great frost in 1739[13] followed by famine and disease, and Gordon states that in 1740 the mortality caused by scanty and improper food was

very high.[14] There was a failure of the potato crop in
1756-7.[15] Then there were the very high rents and the
consequent increase in tithes.[16] After the siege of
Derry, rents were low. Leases were granted on easy
terms, for landlords were eager to get tenants;[17] but
when these leases ran out, the rents were raised to an
exorbitant figure.[18] Finally, about fifty years after
the emigration began, the leases on Lord Donegall's
estate expired, and the rents were then so greatly
advanced that thousands of tenants were unable to
pay them. The tenants were evicted in great numbers,
and these Antrim evictions resulted in a wholesale
emigration to North America.[19] They arrived in time
to swell Washington's army, and as Froude puts it:
"the foremost, the most irreconcilable, the most
determined in pushing the quarrel to the last ex-
tremity, were those whom the Bishops and Lord
Donegall and company had been pleased to drive out
of Ulster."[20] We can truly say, then, of these Ulster
emigrants in the 18th century, that it was not of
their own free will they left their native soil. For
various reasons, religious, social, and economic, they
were compelled to go. As Froude says, they were
driven out.[21]

WHEN? 1718-1774

There waits the New Land:
They shall subdue it,
Leaving their sons' sons
Space for the body,
Space for the soul.

As to the emigration itself, we have now to consider
its extent and quality.

The Five Ships

We begin with 1718, for it was in that year that
what had been a tiny trickle became a flowing stream.
In July and August of that year five ships from
Ireland anchored in Boston Harbour. Two of these
probably sailed from Dublin, calling possibly at
Belfast, and taking on board the Rev. William Boyd,
of Macosquin; one of them sailed from Derry; one
from Coleraine; and one from Glasgow and Belfast.
Shortly afterwards there arrived two more ships, one
from Dublin and one from Derry.[22]

These ships carried emigrants from the valley of
the Bann and the valley of the Foyle. The venture
was not without some preparation, for during the
period 1682-1718, several ministers and licentiates
from Ulster crossed to America. Two of these
ministers, the Rev. William Holmes, of Strabane, and
the Rev. Thomas Craighead, of Donegal, went out in
1714, and, through Holmes' son, who was a ship
captain, were in touch with many of their friends in
Ireland.

New Derry

The Rev. William Boyd, of Macosquin, and the Rev.
William Cornwall, of Clogher, came with the emigrants of 1718. In the same year there went out,
amongst others, the Rev. William Elliott, the Rev.
James Woodside, the Rev. James McGregore, and the

Rev. William Tennent. In the following year came the
Rev. James Hillhouse and the Rev. Samuel Young
with two licentiates, John McKinstry and Samuel
Dorrance, to be followed in succeeding years by a
great army of ministers, licentiates and students, who
built up the Presbyterian Church of North America
on the foundation laid previously by Makemie of
Ramelton, and firmly planted its Blue Banner across
the sea. Most notable, however, was the Rev. James
McGregore, of Aghadowey, who was accompanied by
a large section of his congregation. These emigrants
of 1718 founded and settled the township of New
Londonderry in New Hampshire; they settled also at
Worcester; and in a short time they founded
numerous settlements in New Hampshire and Maine.

I do not need to apologise for dealing with these
emigrants of 1718 at some length, for their importance demands it. I wish to draw attention to several
points of interest regarding them.

Their educational standard was remarkably high
for people of their station in the early 18th century.
They were mostly small farmers and labourers who
had been living in a comparatively remote province of
the United Kingdom. They sent out a petition to
Governor Shute before they sailed. 328 Ulstermen
seem to have signed the petition. 315 wrote their
own names. Only 13 signed with their marks.[23]

In the next place their standard of values is clearly
revealed in the building programme of New Derry.
First, the erection of a rude fort for general protec-

tion against Indian attack; second, the erection of a
house of worship for the community; third, the
building of a school; and last of all, houses for
themselves.

Again, the ministers they had with them were a
tribute to their active church membership in
circumstances where such membership is often lightly
regarded. That McGregore's people had their minister
with them is a fact which does not stand by itself.
Dr. Clark of Cahans went to America in 1764, with
300 members of his congregation. Thus the emigrants
were not strangers in a strange land. They went out
as communities, or to join communities, of the same
race and faith.

Moreover, it is interesting to note that they did not
regard themselves as Irish. In fact, nothing infuriated
them more than to be classed as Irish. "It made my
blood boil," said William Smith, "to hear ourselves
called a parcel of Irish."[24] They protested violently
when American people and American officials described them in this way. They were, they said with
great indignation, people of the Scottish nation in
Ulster who had given their strength and substance
and lives to uphold the British connection there, and
it was hard, in this new land, to be identified with the
very people to whom they had always been opposed.[25]

Then again they introduced into New England two
things that were never seen there before—the small
flax spinning wheel, and the Irish potato. Many of
them wintered in Boston city in the first year of their
arrival, and the good ladies of Boston were tremen-

dously intrigued by the strange machines which
seemed inseparable from the Ulster women. Indeed,
to watch the spinning became a fashionable fad.
Further, it is because of these emigrants that our
potatoes, which came to Europe from South America,
are known as Irish potatoes all over the United
States. A family named Young, from Burt, in
Donegal, presented a few of these strange tubers to
its New England neighbours, but the gift was regarded as poisonous, and the potatoes were thrown
into the nearest swamp. Eventually a man named
Walker, in Andover, Massachusetts, was persuaded
to plant a few tubers. They blossomed and produced
their seed in what we call potato "apples." Mrs.
Walker made a valiant effort to cook these apples.
She tried them boiled, and she tried them roasted,
and in the end pronounced them unfit for food. But
the following spring, when Mr. Walker was ploughing
his garden, he turned up some potatoes, and when
these had been cooked, the verdict was enthusiastic.
Last year I asked an American soldier from Iowa if
his people had a special name to distinguish our
potato from the sweet potato. "Yes," he said, "we
have. We call your kind Irish potatoes."[26]

It need hardly be said that these emigrants of 1718
were a tough people. They were settled on the Indian
border, and were an efficient protection to the province, which was what they were intended to be, and
was, indeed, the reason why they were at first
welcomed by the earlier colonists. They were a terror
to the Indians, and they soon gained a reputation for

fighting and pugnacity that often left them in bad odour with the Quakers and the State Authorities. It is recorded of the New Derry men that their arrival and settlement on the frontier were resented by some colonists nearby, who organised an expedition to drive out the newcomers by force. When these people arrived at the edge of the clearing, they found the Ulster emigrants assembled for worship, their minister in the midst. One good look was sufficient. There was no attack. Very quietly they made for home, and I have no doubt it was the best of their play.[27]

July the First at Oldbridge town
There was a famous battle.

For it was not for nothing that the new township was called Londonderry. Many of the settlers were veterans of the famous siege,[28] and that siege was one of their proudest memories. It is recorded that the song most frequently sung round their firesides was the ballad of the Boyne Water.[29] Oldish men who had starved and fought on Derry walls, and youngish men reared in the Derry tradition were not men to be trifled with.

Their minister was the Rev. James McGregore, a Derry veteran himself. It was his boast that he had fired the great gun which announced the coming of the relief ships. On his death, he was succeeded by the Rev. Matthew Clark, of Boveedy, another Derry soldier, who bore the scar of a siege wound on his temple all his life after.[30]

Priest and teacher of the town,
Long as stands good Londonderry,
With its stories sad and merry,
Shall thy name be handed down
As a man of prayer and mark,
Grave and reverend Matthew Clark.
> *Londonderry (N.H.) Celebration, 1869.*

It was recently said of James McGregore that there was no minister of that name in Derry during the siege. But, like his successor in New Derry, he was a soldier before he became a minister. They can still show you in New Derry the musket that he took with him into his pulpit, while the worshippers took theirs into the pews. They can still tell you that when Matthew Clark lay dying in New Hampshire he directed that none should touch his coffin or carry it to the grave except the men who had fought beside him on Derry walls.[31]

Dear light of purity that gleams for ever
*   Where the wild rain sweeps northward out to sea;—*
That is the Maiden City by the river,
*   And there for us the strength of love shall be.*
> *A. Close.*

It was of such stuff that these men were made, and as time went on, they reared sons that inherited their own adventurous spirit. Their numbers increased. Prof. Perry, of Williams College, Mass., states that in 1734, only fifteen years after the first settlement, the church records in New Derry state that there were 700 communicants present in the

church on Sacrament Sunday. And new settlements
were continually hiving off. During the quarter
century before the Revolution, ten distinct settlements
were made by people from New Derry, and all of these
became towns of influence and importance in New
Hampshire. During the same period two strong
settlements were made in Vermont and one in Maine,
besides numerous families, singly and in groups, in all
directions, North and East especially, and up the
Connecticut river, and over the ridge of the Green
Mountains.[32]

Prof. Perry's statements that neither the Crown
nor the colonies ever appealed to them in vain for
soldiers, and that not a route to Ticonderoga or Crown
Point but was tramped again and again by these
hardy settlers—these statements have abundant
verification. They were with Col. Williams at Lake
George in 1755; they were with Howe and Aber-
crombie at Ticonderoga in 1758; they were with
Amherst at Crown Point in 1759. They were well
represented with Wolfe on the Plains of Abraham at
Quebec.[33]

And so also in the War of Independence. Major
Gen. John Stark, of New Derry, fought from Bunker
Hill till the end of the war, and, in 1781, he was
commander-in-chief of the Northern Department of
the United States Army. He was the son of an Ulsterman, who came to New Derry in 1719. Seventy men
from New Derry went with him to the battle of
Bennington, and the Rev. James McGregore's grandson was an officer on his staff.[34]

General Reid, of New Derry, held a command in the New Hampshire forces all through the war. He was at Bunker Hill, Long Island, White Plains, Trenton, Brandywine, Germanstown, Stillwater and Saratoga. He was with Washington in Valley Forge. He was with Sullivan's expedition against the Six Nations. He was in chief command at Albany in the last summer of the war, and later he commanded all the forces of his State.[35]

General James Millar, of New Derry stock,[36] is said to have brought more reputation out of the war of 1812 than any other American except Winfield Scott, who lived to command all the Northern forces in the Civil War. Nathaniel Hawthorne, in his best known book, "The Scarlet Letter," said that General Millar was New Hampshire's most distinguished soldier.[37] The State of New York presented him with a sword of honour at the end of the war. The United States Congress gave him a gold medal. He was Governor of Arkansas. He was the son of James, the son of Samuel, the son of Robert, one of the first Ulster settlers in New Derry.[38]

Major Robert Rogers, of New Derry,[39] commanded the famous Rangers raised in New Hampshire in 1756, the forerunners of the gallant band of riflemen that fought the British so valiantly under Morgan in the War of Independence. It is interesting to note that the Rangers, who were in the beginning companies of Home Guard raised to protect the settlers against the Indians, and, later, rifle companies in the British service, are once again fighting alongside

British troops in Italy. Most of Rogers' men in 1756
were from his own district in New Hampshire, and of
the same Ulster stock. My readers can remember
that as they watch his exploits and theirs in that
famous picture—North-West Passage. The film is a
strange jumble, and some of it is reminiscent of the
later expedition of George Rodgers Clarke, but as it
is presented, it can only be related to Rogers of New
Hampshire.

But into every walk of life this town of New Derry
and its offspring towns sent out men of distinction,
men like Matthew Thornton,[40] signatory to the Declaration of Independence, and Horace Greeley,
founder of the *New York Tribune,* and a national
figure in the anti-slavery agitation. In fifty years of
New Hampshire history, nearly half of its State
Governors had the Ulster blood,[41] while all through
New England the Ulstermen rapidly forced their way
to the front, and the Puritan and the Quaker were
left behind in the race for fame.

All this, however, merely proves that in 1718 there
was an important emigration from Ulster which had
far-reaching results in New England. I have still to
prove that the emigration persisted on an extensive
scale throughout the 18th century.

In the spring of 1718, an Ulster minister wrote to
a friend in Scotland as follows: " There is like to be
a great desolation in the Northern parts of this
kingdom by the removal of several of our brethren

to the American plantations. No less than six ministers have demitted their congregations, and great numbers of their people go with them."[42]

This testimony is confirmed by Archbishop King in a letter to the Archbishop of Canterbury at the same time. He says: " Your Parliament is destroying what little trade is left us. These and other discouragements are driving away the few Protestants that are left us: insomuch that some thousands of families are gone to the West Indies."[43]

Again, in 1728, the Rev. William Livingston writes of the way in which the people are being driven out of the country to America by want, high rents, and exorbitant tithes. In the same year Archbishop Boulter, in a letter to the Secretary of State in England, goes into greater detail. He states that " it is certain that above 4,200 men, women, and children have been shipped within three years, and of these above 3,100 last summer. The whole North is in a ferment, and people every day are engaging one another to go next year. The humour has spread like a contagious distemper, and the people will hardly bear anyone who tries to cure them of their madness."[44] In the following year he writes again: " The humour of going to America still continues. There are now seven ships at Belfast that are carrying off about 1,000 passengers thither."[45]

James Logan was an Ulsterman from Lurgan. He was a man of great eminence in Pennsylvania. At one time and another he was Provincial Secretary,

President of the Council, Chief Justice of the Supreme
Court, Chief Justice of the Court of Common Pleas,
Mayor of Philadelphia, Recorder of Philadelphia and
Governor of Pennsylvania—not a bad record for an
Ulsterman in his new country.[46] His remarks on the
emigration are dated 1725. "It looks as if Ireland
were to send all her inhabitants. If they continue to
come they will make themselves Proprietors of the
Province. Last week there were no less than six
ships, and every day two or three."[47] Logan was a
Quaker, and no great friend to his fellow-countrymen.
He and the Quakers really seem to have believed that
the Ulstermen, if they continued to come, would
devour the whole country. The Quaker policy, therefore, according to some Ulster-born cynics of later
date, was to get the newcomers away to the Indian
border as quickly as possible, where their love of
fighting would make them useful. The Quaker mer-
chants would sell them (and the Indians) the gun-
powder, and if some of the emigrants were killed,
what matter? They were only a set of turbulent
Irishmen.

But however this might be, the emigration continued. Proud's History of Pennsylvania states that
by 1729 some 6,000 Scotch-Irish had come over, and
for several years prior to 1750 about 12,000
annually.[48] In September, 1736, one thousand families
sailed from Belfast alone.[49]

The same story is told in Baird's History of
Religion in America, Harrison's "The Scot in Ulster,"
and Hodge's Constitutional History of the Presby-

terian Church in America. Indeed so serious was the
shape of things at home that as early as 1728 the
Presbyteries in Ulster were asked to report un-
officially to the Government on the causes of the
emigration, and were exhorted to use their influence
to keep the people at home.[50]

But the emigration went on. Johnson, in his history
of Emigration from the United Kingdom to North
America (London, 1913, p. 2) quotes figures from The
Gentleman's Magazine of 1774 to show that "in the
five years 1769-1774, no less than 43,720 people sailed
from the five Ulster ports of Londonderry, Belfast,
Newry, Larne, and Portrush to various settlements
on the Atlantic seaboard. These points of departure
were thus responsible for an annual outgoing of at
least 8,740 souls." An eminent American historian[51]
writes that between 1730 and 1770, at least half a
million souls were transferred from Ulster to the
colonies, while Froude says that in the two years
which followed the Antrim evictions 30,000 Protestants left Ulster.

Lecky's verdict is as follows: "For nearly three-
quarters of a century this drain on the energetic
Protestant population continued. The famine of 1740
and 1741 gave an immense impulse to the movement,
and it is said that for several years the Protestant
emigrants from Ulster annually amounted to about
12,000."[52] More than 30 years later, Arthur Young
found the stream still flowing, and he tells us that, in
1773, 4,000 emigrants sailed from Belfast.[53] Ap-
proaching the subject from another angle, a modern

American writer estimates that in the three years from 1771 to 1773, at least 100 ships were regularly engaged with emigrant traffic from the North of Ireland.

It is also significant that while in 1701 the population of the State of Pennsylvania is reckoned at 20,000, in less than 50 years it was 250,000. To what was this enormous increase due, if not to an enormous emigration from Scotland and Ulster? No matter where you read in the history of that period, you find the indications of that enormous emigration. Spencer's History of the United States, for example, tells us that in one fortnight in 1773, 3,500 emigrants from Ulster landed at the port of Philadelphia.

These facts, I venture to say, make clear what I set out to prove, that there was a continual flow of emigrants from Ulster to North America in the 18th century, and that this emigration was in numbers amply sufficient to make possible a great Ulster contribution to American progress and United States independence.

Where?

*Something hidden, Go and find it. Go and look
    behind the Ranges.*
*Something lost behind the Ranges. Lost and waiting
    for you. Go!*

The next point to consider is—where did all these people go to after their arrival in America? Some of them, as we have seen, went to Pennsylvania and

New Hampshire, and to the New England States.
Others went south, by sea and land, to Virginia, to
the Carolinas, and to Georgia. All of them had one
thing in common: they were the pioneers on the road
to the West. They had no notion of settling down in
East Coast towns to be navvies and labourers,
politicians, publicans and policemen. The Ulsterman's
urge was towards the backwoods and the Indian
border. President Theodore Roosevelt in his
" Episodes from the Winning of the West " writes:
" It is doubtful if we have fully realised the part
played by this stern and virile people. They formed
the kernel of that American stock who were the
pioneers of our people in their march westward."[54]
And Charles Hanna, in his work on the Scotch-Irish,
refers to them as "that indomitable race, whose
pioneers in unbroken ranks from Champlain to
Florida formed the advance guard of civilisation in
its progress to the Mississippi, and first conquered,
subdued and planted the wilderness between."

These Ulstermen, indeed, went far afield. They
went out to Western Pennsylvania, and to Pittsburg,
of which a member of Congress was able to say not so
long ago: " It is Scotch-Irish in substantial origin,
in complexion, and history—Scotch-Irish in the
countenances of the living and in the records of the
dead."[55] They went from Pennsylvania up the valley
of the Shenandoah, and down the Holston river into
Tennessee. A native of the latter State has declared:
"An overwhelming majority of the early settlers
of our State was Scotch-Irish. Every Tennesseean

descending from our first settlers is to be put down
as of this people if he cannot prove his descent to be
otherwise. No Church other than theirs, the Presbyterian Church, was founded in East Tennessee for
sixty years after its first settlement."[56]

In the Valley of Virginia, as in the Valley of
Cumberland, the Ulsterman were in overwhelming
numbers. Thomas Jefferson, United States President,
said that the Irish held the valley between the Blue
Ridge and the North Mountain, and that they formed
a barrier there which none could venture to leap. You
can read about that in Mary Johnston's novel, " The
Great Valley." They went on through Virginia in
great numbers to the Carolinas. In 1736 Henry
McCullock, an Ulsterman, was granted 64,000 acres in
North Carolina, and to these lands he brought
between 3,000 and 4,000 of his countrymen.[57] The
historian of South Carolina[58] says that there was no
country gave them so many of their inhabitants as
Ireland. The historian of Georgia[59] says that its
prosperity is largely due to the Ulster people and
their descendants, and from them, he adds, the blood
was scattered throughout the South and South-
Western States. " Kentucky was first settled by
Ulstermen from Virginia and North Carolina. East
of the Alleghany Mountains they formed the protect-
ing wall between the red men and the tide-water.
But not for long did our people endure the mountain
frontier. Everywhere they leaped across it, and
opened out the country in the West "—thus Governor
Gilmer of Georgia.

I have mentioned Rogers' Rangers and " North-West Passage." Many of my readers will have seen another well-known picture, " Sergeant Yorke," which gives a glimpse of life in the border country between Kentucky and Tennessee. It adds interest to that picture to know that the people there are largely of Ulster stock, that they retain some remnant of Ulster speech, and that of such people is Daniel Boone, the Indian Scout and fighter. His memory is still cherished in that region, as the picture testifies, and his name is the greatest to be found in the long annals of American frontiersmen.

But the mountain region from Pennsylvania to Kentucky has perhaps a less worthy interest for us in Northern Ireland. These mountains once harboured a rebellion which it took a United States army to put down, and the rebellion occurred because the authorities tried to stop the making of untaxed poteen.[60] The industry, we are told, still flourishes in out of the way places. It is to be feared that we exported it with the spinning wheels and the potatoes.

Ulster's mark on America is also visible in its place names. There are eighteen towns in the United States named after Belfast. There are seven Derrys, nine Antrims, and sixteen Tyrones. There is a Coleraine in Massachusetts. New Hampshire has Stewartstown. Washington, Ohio, and Iowa have each a Pomeroy. Hillsborough is in New Hampshire, Illinois, North Dakota, and Wisconsin. Maine has Newry. Ohio has Banbridge. In twelve States there are twelve Mil-

fords. In Michigan there is a town named after that
river that is not in Ulster, but was once dyed red with
Ulster blood, the famous River Boyne.

THE ULSTER-AMERICAN ACHIEVEMENT

We have now traced our countrymen across the
ocean. We have seen that they crossed in very large
numbers and over a long period of years. We have
seen something of their distribution in the American
Colonies. It remains now to deal with the further
question, What did they do? What was the nature
of their contribution to the United States?

The Road to the West

In the first place they led the way to the West.
It was they who steadily pushed the frontier back,
over the Alleghanies and on to the Mississippi. That
is agreed. Theodore Roosevelt is emphatic on this
point, and he was a man of action, with a spirit akin
to that of the Ulster pioneers. He is, however, only
one voice out of many to tell the same story, and to
argue the matter further would only be waste of time,
since Ulster's pre-eminence on the frontier is a
common-place of American history. And indeed, were
argument required, it would be almost enough to
mention the names of Danied Morgan of Ranger fame,
who was born at Ballynascreen, of Robert Rogers of
New Derry and his Rangers, of George Rodgers
Clarke, who more than any other man secured the
North-West Territory for the United States,[61] and of

such famous Indian scouts as Simon Kenton,[62] Davy
Crockett, and Danny Boone.[63]

The Revolution

But their record on the frontier was rivalled by
their valour at the war of the Revolution. They
were eager to fight in that war, and they were the
first to proclaim it. Here is what President McKinley
said about them in 1893: " They were the first
to proclaim for freedom in these United States:
even before Lexington the Scotch-Irish blood had been
shed for American freedom. In the forefront of every
battle was seen their burnished mail, and in the
rear of retreat was heard their voice of constancy."[64]
There was very little " burnished mail " in Washington's ragged army, and the General's lip would have
curled at such flowers of rhetoric in such a connexion;
but he would have been the first to admit the truth
below the rhetoric—the courage, the steadfast
loyalty, the unshakeable determination and fighting
quality of his soldiers of Ulster origin and descent.
The reference by President McKinley to the Ulster
blood shed before Lexington is explained by the fact
that the first encounter between British and
Americans was not at Concord and Lexington, but on
the Alamance river in North Carolina on May the
14th, 1771, between the Ulster-Irish of that region
and a British force under Governor Tryon.[65]

The well-known American historian Bancroft is no
less emphatic than McKinley. " The first voice

publicly raised in America to dissolve all connection with Great Britain came, not from the Puritans of New England, nor from the Dutch of New York, nor from the Cavaliers of Virginia, but from the Scotch-Irish Presbyterians."[66] The reference here, as in McKinley, is to the Mecklenburg Resolutions of Independence.[67] These Resolutions were adopted by a convention of Ulster-Irish which met in North Carolina some time before the issue of the well-known Declaration drafted by Jefferson. The Resolutions were drafted and proposed by Dr. Ephraim Brevard, of Huguenot-Ulster descent. The convention was summoned by Thomas Polk, whose forbears came from the Donegal border to found one of the great families of America. Up till a short time ago in Ulster, the surname Pollock was almost invariably pronounced Polk (Poke), but to-day there seems to be little relish either for the pronounciation or for this written form of the name. Yet a President of the United States, several American Generals, and many distinguished men, including one who was both a general and a bishop, preferred the name with its original sound, and have left it laurelled with distinction.

A similar Declaration of Independence was issued by the people of Ulster origin and descent in New Hampshire, and this Declaration also preceded the Declaration of Congress.[68] President Theodore Roosevelt referred to these Ulster-Irish Declarations when he said: " The West was won by those who have been rightly called the Roundheads of the South, the same men who before any other declared for American independence."[69]

The Army

Throughout the whole war General Washington made no concealment of his high regard for the American troops of Ulster origin. He vowed that if the worst came to the worst, he would fight his last battle by their side. Other troops came and went, and sometimes his army was small, but small or great, a large proportion of it had the Ulster blood, the Ulster tenacity of spirit, the Ulster determination to see a thing right through till the end. "If defeated everywhere else," said this great leader, "I will make my last stand for liberty among the Scotch-Irish of my native Virginia." Dr. Mackintosh, in an address to a Scotch-Irish Congress, has described these soldiers of our race in words that are strictly true: "At Derry, at Valley Forge, at King's Mountain and at Brandywine, the first to start and the last to quit."

As to their actual numbers in the American army, an American writer of that period asserts that up to the coming of the French, Ireland had furnished troops in the ratio of 100 to 1 of any other nation.[70] There is good reason to believe that, during the war, the Ulster-Irish formed one-third of the total population. The writer's estimate of our troops engaged is probably extravagant, but it may have been true at certain periods of the war, and especially true at times of the regulars as distinct from the militia. It is well known that the record of Congress in the war was far from creditable. It would not give Washington enough regular troops, and it would not properly equip, clothe or feed the troops that he had. Those who do not wish to read about this in history can read about it in the American novel "Rabble in Arms." Congress wanted to fight the war on the cheap, with militia; it feared to demand long-term service; it pandered to complaints; it was fertile ground for military intrigue; it let Washington down again and again. He had many claims to greatness; but among them this must never be forgotten, that he was able to keep an army in the field when a lesser man would have thrown up his command in disgust. Militia, here to-day, and away to-morrow, were no substitute for troops of the line, yet again and again the general's appeals for more regulars fell on deaf ears. There were times, therefore, when his army was small, and since it is generally agreed that the Ulster-Irish were steadfastly enthusiastic for the war, it could very well be that often they comprised the greater part of his men. One famous force of regulars was the Pennsylvania Line, and these were Ulster-Irish almost to a man.[71]

Indeed, all the evidence we can obtain confirms the predominance of our people in the army and in the war effort. Joseph Galloway was a delegate to the first Continental Congress, but he became bitterly pro-British, and sailed for England. He appeared before a Committee of the British House of Commons and was asked "What were the troops in the service of Congress chiefly composed of?" He replied "I can

answer the question with precision. There were
scarcely one quarter of them natives of America. Half
of them were Irish. The other quarter was English
and Scotch." Before the same Committee, and in
answer to the same question, Major-General Robert-
son said: " I remember General Lee, the American
general, telling me that half the rebel army was
from Ireland."[72]

Prior to the election of the first Congress, the only
assembly that covered the whole country, or was in
any sense representative of it, was the General Synod
of the Presbyterian Church. In 1775 it met in Philadelphia, side by side with the new Congress of the
States. Congress seemed to hesitate, but a Pastoral
Letter issued by the Synod to all its congregations
is reckoned to have been the chief cause which led
the colonies to resistance at that time.[73] It is recorded, moreover, that the Governors of the Central
and Southern colonies informed the home Government that the Presbyterian clergy were to blame for
the oncome of the Revolution, and for inflaming the
people towards rebellion.[74] Now since the great
majority of Presbyterian clergy and people were
either of Ulster origin or Ulster descent, we have here
the clearest of testimony to the enthusiasm of Ulster-
Americans for the war effort. Plowden states that
" most of the successes in America were immediately
owing to the vigour and courage of the Irish emigrants."[75] And it is clear that a similar impression
must have prevailed in England, for Lord Mountjoy
said in the House of Commons " We have lost America

through the Irish"; and how else can you explain
Horace Walpole's famous jibe to the Cabinet? "I hear
that our American cousin has run away with a
Scotch-Irish parson."

Readers will note the frequent mention of "Irish"
and "Ireland" in the last two paragraphs. They can
be quite certain that the words are of limited applica-
tion, and that in all cases their meaning should be
narrowed down. Those who used the words used them
because they had an imperfect appreciation of the
situation in Ireland, and because by this time the
Ulster indignation at being classed as "Irish" had
largely vanished. But it cannot be denied that the
use of the wider terms has caused much misapprehen-
sion, so that, even in America, Ireland as a whole
has been given credit which is not justly her due.
In this way a handle has been given to Irish and
Irish-American agitators which they have not been
slow to use, and which is still used, in total disregard
of historical accuracy.

Yet! Freedom, yet; thy banners torn but flying,
Stream, like the thunderstorm against the wind.

Let me pass on now to a few of the exploits of our
people in the war. There was a battle fought at King's
Mountain, in South Carolina; and it is a moderate
estimate to reckon half the population of that State
as of Ulster origin at that time. Things were looking
black just then, and even Washington's brave spirit
seemed to quail. "This is a dark hour," he wrote,

" and I don't know what is to become of us."[76] In this battle, a body of American militia—we might call them Home Guard—after a forced march of four days, attacked and defeated a British force of twice its size, killed the British commander and 180 of his men, and took upwards of 1,000 prisoners. The five colonels in the American force were Presbyterian elders, and the troops they commanded were of the same race and faith. Washington and Jefferson said that this battle was the turning point of the war. [77]

Or take the battle of Cowpens. Daniel Morgan was in command, with a mixed force of regulars, militia, and dragoons. He and his men killed 100 British, wounded 200, and took 500 prisoners with a large quantity of military stores. These numbers sound small in our ears, but no large armies were engaged in this war, and figures like these represented a crushing British defeat. For this victory, Congress gave General Morgan a gold medal, General Pickens a sword of honour, and Colonel Howard a silver medal. Morgan and Pickens were elders of the Presbyterian Church, and all three, as well as the troops they commanded, were Ulster-Irish.[78]

These were victories which were not typical of the war. That war dragged on year after year with few victories and many defeats. The British lost it because, for a short time, they lost command of the sea. They lost it because the Government clung to vain hopes of settlement by negotiation and was vigorous in its prosecution only by fits and starts. The view that it was carried on merely to please the

King has no basis in history; and there is much
evidence to shew that the bulk of the people at home
approved the war or were indifferent to it. But the
Government was hampered by a formidable anti-war
party in Parliament, a party that was formidable
not because of its numbers, but because of its
eloquence and ability. Yet in none of these considera-
tions, temporary loss of sea power, sluggish general-
ship, or Parliamentary opposition, is there the fact of
first moment. We lost the war because year after
year General Washington and his ragged army
appeared in the field and refused to disappear. It is
true that we would have escaped defeat at Yorktown
if the Navy and the transports had been in time. But
this would only have meant defeat postponed. No
nation could have finally conquered America. No
nation can finally conquer a people that keeps its
soul, and is determined in resistance.

A few words may be said here about the civil side
of the war effort. In 1780 the army of the United
Colonies was in sad condition, imperfectly supplied
with equipment and munitions of war, disgracefully
clad, and poorly fed. A number of patriotic citizens,
hopeless of Congress action, subscribed a large sum
of money to purchase equipment, clothing and food
for their fighting men. Among these patriots was
Blair McClenaghan, who gave 50,000 dollars. He was
born in Ulster. James Mease gave 25,000 dollars. He
was born in Strabane. His uncle John, born in the
same town, gave 20,000 dollars. John Dunlop gave a
similar sum, and he also was born in Strabane. John

Murray was born in Belfast. He gave 30,000 dollars. John Donaldson, of Dungannon, gave 10,000 dollars. John Nixon, Thomas Barclay and John Nesbitt were three men of Ulster origin who gave 30,000 dollars apiece. This list could be extended, and these are only a few out of those who might be named. The acid test of enthusiasm for a cause is generous support in the form of hard cash. It is clear that our folk passed the test.[79]

Here come the heroes, their earthly travail over,
Bent shields and bloody banners left behind.

                                A. Close.

Nothing, however, brings more conviction of the great part played by our people in the Revolution than to consider the numbr of American officers of high distinction who were of Ulster origin or descent.

General Richard Montgomery was born near Convoy in County Donegal. He fell while gallantly leading his men in an attack on Quebec. By a strange coincidence, the British commander on that occasion, and the man who saved Canada for the British Empire, was General Sir Guy Carleton, who was born near Strabane, only a few miles from Montgomery's home. The two generals were old acquaintances who had served together in the British army.[80]

General Henry Knox has been described as, after Washington, the most illustrious soldier of the Revolution. He was from New Derry, and was the son of an emigrant from Donegal. He was the

organiser and commander of the American artillery
arm, and he fought in every battle of the war. He
was dearer to Washington than any other man. In
that most moving scene at Fraunces Tavern on 4th
December, 1783, when Washington said farewell to
his officers, Henry Knox was the first officer to get
the farewell greeting, and both men were in tears.
He was the Secretary for War in Washington's first
Cabinet.

General Anthony Wayne's grandfather fought
under King William at the Boyne. He was a great
cavalry leader, and a fierce fighting general of
infantry who told Washington he would storm hell
if he got the orders.[81] A few years ago a friend in
Philadelphia wrote to me that he had just been
watching a street procession organised by the
Knights of Columbus and the Ancient Order of
Hibernians. At the head of the procession was a
banner, and on this banner was a painting of General
Wayne, grandson of a Boyne soldier. It is in this
way that our laurels are stolen without scruple and
without shame.

General Andrew Lewis was born in Donegal, and
at one time it looked as if he would become Commander-in-Chief of the American army. General Dan
Morgan was born at Ballynascreen, in County Derry.
The British General Burgoyne said to him after the
battle of Saratoga: " Your Scotch-Irish Rifles is the
finest in the world."[82] Bancroft pronounced him the
ablest commander of Light Troops in the world, and
affirmed that in no European army of that day were

there troops like those he had trained.[83] I was happy to have as a frequent visitor to my home last year* Major Murray, who now commands, in the Middle East, a battalion of Rangers which has already added fresh renown to laurels that once crowned Rogers of New Derry and Morgan of Ballynascreen.

General Walter Stewart was born in Ulster in the city of Derry.[54] General Thomas Robinson went out from Ulster just before the war. He was Anthony Wayne's brother-in-law. General William Thompson and his famous brother Charles were born in Maghera.[85] General Enoch Poor was born of Ulster parents in New Hampshire.[86] General John Stark was born in New Derry.[87] General William Maxwell[88] was born in Ulster. General John Clark was born in Antrim.[89] General Andrew Pickens was born in Pennsylvania of Ulster parents.[90] General Ephraim Blaine was born in Donegal. He was Washington's quartermaster. General Thomas Polk's people had been in America for 100 years before the war, but the original emigrant came from Ulster. Some records state that he came from Derry, and others that he came from Donegal: his probable birthplace was on the border between these two counties.[91] General James Miller was from New Derry and so also was General George Reid.[92] General George Rodgers Clarke was born in the valley of Virginia.[93] He was of Ulster forbears, and was one of the most distinguished officers in the American army. The

* 1942.

American novelist, Winston Churchill, has much to say about this officer in " The Crossing."

General Joseph Reed was the son of Ulster parents who settled in New Jersey. He was Washington's adjutant-general.[94] General James Clinton was an Ulsterman who won distinction by his defence of Fort Clinton in 1777. His brother George was Governor of New York for 18 years, and was twice Vice-President of the United States.[95] General John Armstrong was born in Ulster.[96] General James Ewing, General William Henry, and General Rutherford were all of Ulster descent.[97] General Michael Simpson was an Ulsterman who served under Montgomery at Quebec. General William Irvine was born at Enniskillen. He raised the 6th Pennsylvania Regiment, and commander the troops on the N.W. frontier. The father of General Francis Preston was born in Ulster, and the general's father-in-law was General William Campbell, one of the five Presbyterian colonels at the battle of King's Mountain.[98]

In the city of Savannah there is a splendid monument to the memory of Sergeant William Jasper, and one of the principal squares in that city bears his name. That name is still glowing with distinction in America, and it is in every history of the war. He was born in Ulster.[99]

General George Croghan was in the war of 1812. To guess his origin and faith is easy, for his mother was a sister of General George Rodgers Clarke. He received the thanks of Congress, a gold medal, and a

sword of honour. There is a State monument to his
memory in Ohio.[100]

Finally, without taking this list further, there is
Andrew Jackson, President of the United States,
General in the war of 1812, victor at New Orleans,
and by-named Old Hickory then and forever. He was
born in North Carolina shortly after his Ulster
parents had arrived in America.

This is something of our military record in the
war of the Revolution and the was of 1812. There is
no other race in the United States than can produce a
Roll of Honour so long and so shining with distinction. Add to it the colonels and majors and captains
of this race, the sergeants, riflemen, troopers and
gunners, add to it the Ulster-Irish in the Navy, and
who shall deny our claim to have done more, much
more than any others to make the United States?
Washington's own tribute was emphatic, not only in
words that I have quoted, but in deeds. After the
war he was presented with a large sum of money as
a personal gift from the American public. He gave
this money, in its entirety, to found a school and
college in that part of Virginia which was packed
with Ulster-Irish.[101]

The Civil War

The Civil War was the greatest and bloodiest war
ever fought on American soil. But since it is outside
the period with which we are most concerned, and
does not belong to the making of the United States,
it must have only a passing reference. A few names

may be mentioned, indicative of what might be presented if it were necessary or desirable.

The Commander-in-Chief of the Northern Army at the end of the war was Ulysses Grant, later President of the United States. His mother was the descendant of an Ulsterman who settled in Pennsylvania. The soldier of greatest reputation in the North for a considerable part of the war was General George B. McClellan, sometimes called " the pocket Napoleon." He was the descendant, on both sides of the house, of Ulster settlers of 1718. So also was General McPherson, of whom Grant said at his death: " The country has lost one of its best soldiers, and I have lost my best friend." General Irvin McDowell's ancestor was a settler of 1718, who had fought in the siege of Dery. To these names may be added those of Sam Houston, the maker of Texas, of General Halpine, whose father was an Irish rector, and of General James Shields, who was born near Pomeroy, and was the only man who ever defeated Stonewall Jackson in battle or skirmish. It is proper to state here that General Shields was not of "planter" stock, but of the ancient race and faith. [102]

The military leadership of the South was brilliant, and the ranks were filled with men of Ulster stock in the grey uniforms of the Confederates; but it must suffice here to mention the names of three important leaders: General (and Bishop) Leonidas Polk, whose ancestor came from Derry or Donegal; General J. E. B. Stuart, whose great-great-grandfather was born in Derry city; and finally the name of that famous Blue

Light elder, whose piety and valour and military
genius surround a lost cause with undying lustre, and
who might well be classed with John Nicholson as a
thunderbolt of war—the mighty name of Stonewall
Jackson.[103]

On the Confederate side, North Carolina, home of
the Ulster-Irish, led all the Southern States in enlisted
men, and in killed and wounded. In the North, the
pre-eminence goes to Pennsylvania, peopled in great
measure by folk with the Ulster blood. The bloodiest
single conflict of the war was fought between two
regiments at Gettysburg, the 26th North Carolina
Regiment and the 151st Pennsylvania Regiment.
Both regiments were practically wiped out. Well
might Colonel Johnston say in 1889: " The greatest
losses in the war occurred when the iron soldiers of
North Carolina and Pennsylvania, descendants of the
same race and stock, met on the field of battle, and
locked arms in the embrace of death." [104] And to this
tribute may be added that of one whose verdict will
be questioned by few. The Rev. Dr. David Macrea, a
Scots minister, on a visit to America, interviewed
the great Commander of the Confederate Forces,
General Robert E. Lee, and asked him, " What race
do you believe makes the best soldiers? " General
Lee answered: " The Scotch who came to this country
by way of Ireland." Dr. Macrea asked him, " Why
do you say that, General? " " Because," replied this
great soldier, " they have all the dash of the Irish in
taking a position, and all the stubbornness of the
Scotch in holding it."

The fighting quality of Ulstermen has not deteriorated since this tribute was paid to it by Robert Lee. On the 1st July, 1916, the 36th Ulster Division went into battle on the Somme. The Ulster spear-head pierced the German defences for two miles. Half the Division was left on the battlefield, but it advanced farther than any other unit in the battle, and captured the fifth line of German trenches. The Commanding Officer of the Division said that nothing finer had been done in the war. The *Times* correspondent wrote that, as he watched the attack, he felt he would rather be an Ulsterman than anything else in the world. Conan Doyle, in his history of British campaigns in France and Flanders, declares that " all soldiers would agree that, among all these heroes of the Somme, there was not one which could at its highest claim more than equality of achievement that day with the men of Ulster."

And these men, be it remembered, were not conscripts but volunteers, as are also the tens of thousands in the forces now. Ulstermen in North Africa and Italy, as well as in the retreat to Dunkirk, on the high seas, and in the air, have fully maintained a great fighting tradition; and such names as Alexander, Montgomery, Brooke, Auchinleck, and Dill testify to the superb quality of Ulster general-ship in the present war.

Hushed are their battlefields, ended their marches,
Deaf are their ears to the drum-beat of morn.

Peace smiles at last; the Nation calls her sons
To sheath the sword; her battle flag she furls.

The Declaration of Independence and the Presidents

Enough, however, of this talk of battles. The Ulster achievement in America is an achievement in peace as well as in war.

The issue of the Declaration of Independence is the most important event in the history of the United States, and one of the notable events in world history. The document itself is in the handwriting of an Ulsterman, Charles Thompson of Maghera, Perpetual Secretary of the Continental Congress, who landed in America as a penniless orphan boy, robbed of all he possessed by a rascally ship-captain. He died, an honoured figure, a man so renowned for uprightness of character that the Delaware Indians named him "the man of truth," and John Adams called him "the life of liberty," and his name became associated with a proverb: "It's as true as if Charles Thompson's name were to it."[105]

The Declaration that was first transcribed by an Ulsterman was also first printed by an Ulsterman, John Dunlap of Strabane. It was first read in public by the son of an Ulsterman, Colonel John Nixon. And the only signature on it for a month was the name of a man whose ancestors were Presbyterians from County Down, John Hancock, President of Congress and Governor of Massachusetts.[106]

Let us take a look at some of the other signatures to this great document.

William Whipple—his parents came to Maine from Ulster in 1730. Robert Paine—his grandfather came from Dungannon. Thomas McKean—his father was born near Ballymoney. Thomas Nelson—his grandfather came from Strabane. Matthew Thornton—his father sailed in one of the five ships in 1718, and settled in New Derry. George Taylor—his father was an Ulster minister. Edward Rutledge—like his great brother John, he was the son of an Ulster emigrant.[107]

This is a respectable representation, and further investigation would probably make it larger. But the list of men of Ulster origin who have held the great office of President of the United States is even more impressive. Up till the present time there have been thirty-one Presidents. Very nearly half of these, either on the paternal or maternal side, have had the Ulster blood: John Adams, John Quincy Adams, James Monroe, Andrew Jackson, James K. Polk, James Buchanan, Andrew Johnson, Ulysses Grant, Chester Arthur, Grover Cleveland, Benjamin Harrison, William McKinley, Theodore Roosevelt, and Woodrow Wilson. Of Vice-Presidents we have Calhoun, Clinton, Wilson, Johnson, Breckinridge, Hendricks and Arthur.[108] The Irish-American vote and influence is a weighty factor in American politics. Yet no Irishman except of Ulster Protestant stock has ever been called to the White House.

John Rutledge was the greatest man ever born in South Carolina. He was the son of an Ulster

emigrant. He was the first Governor of South
Carolina, and was Chief Justice of the Supreme Court
of the United States. He was the Chairman of the
committee of five who made the first draft of the
American Constitution.[109] In his novel " The Carol-
inian," Rafael Sabatini presents a very vivid picture
of this Ulsterman's son.

After the war of the Revolution there were thirteen
States. Of the first Governors of these States, seven
were of Ulster origin. But the name of those of our
race who held high office is legion. There are State
Governors by the hundred and Justices of State
Supreme Courts by the score.

The Church

Oh, who can tell how much we owe to thee,
Makemie, and to labours such as thine,
For all that makes America the shrine
Of faith untrammelled and of conscience free?
Stand here, gray stone, and consecrate the sod
Where sleeps this brave Scots-Irish man of God.

Van Dyke.

The founder of the great American Presbyterian
Church was the Rev. Francis Makemie of Ramelton.[110]
Year after year, the minutes of the Synod of Ulster,
and of the Secession Synod, record the names of
ministers going to America, of licentiates ordained
for America, of licentiates and students removing to
America. In 1760, that is in less than forty years
after the arrival of the Ulster settlers, there were 300

congregations to add to the handful that had been established before their coming.[111] In 1705 there were just seven congregations. A Pennsylvanian minister,[112] writing in 1744, said that " all our congregations except two or three are chiefly made up of people from Ireland."[113] Makemie founded the first Presbytery. The Rev. John Hampton, born at Burt, was the first Moderator of the first Presbyterian Synod. The Rev. John Rodgers, whose father was an Ulsterman from Derry city, was the first Moderator of the first General Assembly.[114] The Rev. Robert Smith, born in Derry city, was the second Moderator.[115] The Rev. George Duffield, son of an Ulster emigrant, was the first Clerk of the first General Assembly.[116] Nearly 300 ministers, of Ulster extraction, are known to have served in the ministry of American Presbyterian Churches in the period 1680-1820. Of these 189 came by way of Ulster. It is unfortunately impossible to give anything like a complete estimate of the total number of ministers of Ulster origin in America in the 18th century, but the list of nearly 250 names in the Appendices is itself a respectable quota.

Education

It must also be said that these people of ours took with them to America that zeal for education that is their heritage from John Knox. They founded schools all over the country. They were pioneers, and their ministers had to be pioneers too. They had to go with their people, and in the wilderness there was no one but the minister qualified to teach the young.

And their schools were not merely elementary
schools; they were also classical academies; and
there is many a noble university to-day, with campus
and college hall, with lecture-rooms and hostels, which
can trace its beginning to the rude log-hut built by an
Ulster minister to school the children in the primæval
forest. They were our people who founded the famed
Log College which gave birth to the great University
of Princetown, and not only to it, but also to Jefferson
College, to Hampden Sidney College, to the University
of North Carolina, the University of Pennsylvania,
and to Washington and Lee University in Virginia.[117]
The founder of Lafayette College was of Ulster stock;
the first President of Bowdoin and the first President
of what became the University of Nashville were of
the same race. No wonder Dr. Hogg of New Jersey
said in 1928: " Ninety per cent. of the primitive
religious, educational, and university work done in
America was done by the Scotch-Irish."

Abolition and the Press

Again, it is commonly believed that the egitation
for the freedom of the slaves began among the
Puritans of Boston and New England. This belief
has no foundation in fact. The agitation began
among the folk from our province. Forty years
before any anti-slavery movement started in New
England, the Reformed Presbyterians of South
Carolina and East Tennessee debarred all slave-
holders from Communion.[118] In 1820 John Rankin
said that it was safer to make Abolition speeches in

Kentucky or Tennessee than in the North. The
speakers at an Abolition meeting in Boston were
mobbed as late as 1833.[119]   And one of the most
active of the Northern Abolitionists was Horace
Greeley, who was from New Derry.

But in every walk of life our people proved their
mettle. Horace Greeley was the founder of the *New
York Tribune*. Robert Bonner, from Ramelton, was
the founder of the *New York Ledger*.   Charles
Halpine, of the same stock, founded the *New York
Citizen*.   John Dunlap, from Strabane, printed the
first daily paper ever issued in the United States.
Edgar Allan Poe's great-grandfather was an Ulsterman.[120]

Of merchant princes, we can claim the Stuarts of
New York, and the Armours of Chicago. Of
financiers, Andrew Mellon, whose link is with New-
townstewart. We have Robert Fulton, of steam-boat
fame, and Morse, the inventor of the Morse system
of telegraphy, and McCormack, the inventor of the
reaping machine. McCormack's ancestors fought in
the siege of Derry. But the time would fail me to
instance the countless further examples of Ulster-
American industry and achievement.

New York is proud of its " first families." Which
of them can compare in eminence and public service
with the Routledges, the Calhouns, the Breckinridges,
the Polks, the McClellans, the McDowells, the Pattons
and the Prestons? The American writer, W. A.
Robinson, thus describes the Prestons, the first of

whom was born in Derry city: " They were governors
and ambassadors and senators; they were college
presidents and eminent divines; they were generals,
and statesmen from Virginia, Kentucky, Louisiana,
Missouri, California, Ohio, New York, Indiana, and
South Carolina. Four of them were Governors of
Virginia. They were members of the Cabinets of
Jefferson, Taylor, Buchanan, and Lincoln. They had
generals by the dozen and senators by the score, and
officers by the hundred. They furnished three
candidates for the Vice-Presidency of the United
States. And all were from this Ulster emigrant from
the city of Derry."

Entirely an Ulster-Irish Achievement

My task is almost done, but there are still some
things that must be said. We are not willing to lose
the credit for these achievements of our people. We
are not willing that this credit should be stolen from
those to whom it belongs, and made part and parcel
of a tireless propaganda for our political extinction.

There are some writers who detail truly, as they
think, and without malicious intent, the contribution
of "Irishmen" to the making of the United States.
But there are others who nurse their anti-Ulster bias
with unremitting care. They set down their half-
truth, knowing that, on challenge, there is a loop-hole
of escape. But to excuse them on the ground that an
Ulsterman is an Irishman is beside the point, for he
might also be truthfully described as a European.
The fair criticism of the half-truth in this instance

is that it misrepresents, and is intended to misrepresent the true facts of the case, that it is the theft of credit from those to whom it belongs, and that it is, in fact and by intention, the covert discharge of political venom.

We are entitled to protest against theft of this kind. We are not to remain dumb when achievements such as have been enumerated in these pages are calmly seized by Irish Republicans, and used as weapons to gain sympathy in America for the Republican cause. We are entitled to protest when Eire politicians and Ulster malcontents make these achievements a springboard for attack on our people. These are the deeds of our kindred and not theirs. This is the record of Protestant Ulster. There were individual Southern Irishmen here and there, and some names of distinction such as Carroll, Barry, Moylan, and Sullivan. Let these and their like be named with honour; but to state facts is not to appeal to religious prejudice, and the fact is that Southern Irishmen made no important contribution to American freedom.

Why? Because they were not there to make it. There was no substantial body of them in America, not even in Maryland. There was no emigration from Southern Ireland, except the tiniest of trickles, till the 19th century.

Consider these facts. It is generally agreed that the population of the United States at the close of the war was slightly over three millions. This population was not compressed in large cities and towns. Philadelphia had little more than half the present population of our Derry. New York and Boston were just big towns slightly larger than our Portadown. Charlestown had about as many people as our Omagh.

Now it is undisputed that in 1784 there were only 20 priests in the whole of the United States from the Atlantic to the Mississippi.[121] How could 20 priests minister to a large fraction of three million people so widely scattered and in such a vast area? Why, in the same area, and at the same time there were at least 200 ministers of Ulster origin; there were ministers from Scotland in large numbers; there were ministers of the Protestant Episcopal Church; there was the great body of Congregationalist ministers; and there were some Methodists and Baptists.

Again, it is undisputed that the first Roman Catholic bishop in the United States was not consecrated till nearly ten years after the last battle of the war.[122] Will anyone believe that the interests of a great Church should have been so strangely neglected as to leave a large fraction of these three million people to this late period without a proper bishop and with only 20 priests?

Bishop England,[123] writing of the period immediately following the war, mentions "the scattered Catholics," and "the few who exercised the ministry." He says that when he came to America in 1820, he saw an estimate of the Roman Catholic population at that time. He refers to it as "a not unfriendly estimate." He declares that it was "from a respectable source." The figure he saw was 100,000. The total population then was ten millions. It is true that Bishop England thought that estimate of his people too low. For our part we need neither accept it nor reject it. That such a figure should be produced at all from a respectable and not unfriendly source is proof sufficient that in the total population the Southern Irish, even 39 years after Yorktown, must have been few and far between.

Yet this same bishop declared, in a statement[124] worthy to be set beside the Nationalist Party letter[125] to President Wilson near the close of the last war, that "the best, the most gallant and hardy portion of the American troops, the Pennsylvania Line, was chiefly composed of Irish Catholics." The bishop's imagination was colossal. The Pennsylvania Line was chiefly composed of Ulster Protestants and the descendants of Ulster Protestants.

Arthur Young was a reliable observer, whose "Tour in Ireland" is a mine of information used by many historians. Writing of this emigration which was still going on during his tour (1780), he declares: "The Catholics never went; they seem not only tied to the country, but almost to the parish in which their ancestors lived."[126] Gordon (History of Ireland, II., 216) has a similar story to tell. Indeed it was just because the emigration was Protestant that several districts in Ulster that were predominantly Protestant are now predominantly Roman Catholic.

President Theodore Roosevelt, in his History of New York, does not mince his words. " It is a curious fact," he says, "that in the Revolutionary war, the Germans and the Catholic Irish should have furnished the bulk of the auxiliaries to the regular English soldiers; but the fiercest and most ardent Americans of all were the Presbyterian Irish settlers and their descendants."[127] And the American Owen Wister is even more outspoken: "Americans are being told in these days that they owe a debt of support to Irish independence, because the Irish fought with us in our own struggle for independence. Yes, the Irish did, and we do owe them a debt of support. But it was the Orange Irish who fought in our Revolution, and not the Green Irish."[128]

Many Americans are misled by Republican propaganda. We ask them to remember to whom it is that they largely owe their freedom; we ask them to remember that it was our people from Ulster who were the first to start and the last to quit; and when appeals are made to them, with reminders of services said to have been rendered, let them remember that these reminders rest on no basis of fact, that Southern Ireland was no more in that war than she is in this one, and that she made no mark on the United States till the 19th century.

Let me emphasise, in closing, that we are not beggars for American help in our own struggle. We shall not rush cablegrams to American Presidents. We shall not beg for a hearing in an American Senate or House of Representatives. We shall not plead for American influence with Britain on our behalf. We can fight our own battle. We can still be the last to quit.

But we do ask that American opinion on the Ulster question should be guided by knowledge and understanding rather than by Republican clamour. We do ask that the American people should thoughtfully and fairly consider the facts, the facts of our position here, and the facts of their own history over there. Knowledge brings understanding, and the child of understanding is sympathy. We ask for all three, and it is we who have the right to ask.

They were Twain when they crossed the sea,
  And often their folk had warred;
But side by side, on the ramparts wide,
  They cheered as the gates were barred:
And they cheered as they passed their King
  To the ford that daunted none,
For, field or wall, it was each for all
  When the Lord had made them One.

Thistle and Rose, they twined them close
  When their fathers crossed the sea,
And they dyed them red, the live and the dead,
  Where the blue-starred lint grows free;
Where the blue-starred lint grows free,
  Here in the Northern sun,
Till His way was plain, He led the Twain,
  And He forged them into One.

They were One when they crossed the sea
  To the land of hope and dream.
Salute them now, whom none could cow,
  Nor hold in light esteem!
Whose footsteps far in peace and war
  Still sought the setting sun!
With a dauntless word and a long bright sword—
  The Twain whom God made One!

APPENDIX

I

(1) Reid: History of the Presbyterian Church in Ireland, III. 221, 222. (2) Mant: History of the Church of Ireland, II. 98. Killen: Ecclesiastical History of Ireland, II. 188, 218, 219. Reid: III. 75, 224. Lecky: History of Ireland in the XVIIIth Century, I. 112, 113. D'Alton: Lives of the Irish Archbishops, 298. (3) Letters of Archbishop Boulter: I. 289, 295. (4) Journals of the Irish House of Commons: vi. 661— Commons' Committee Report. (5) MS. Sermon by the Rev. James McGregor, quoted in Rev. E. L. Parker's History of Londonderry, New Hampshire, in which McGregor declares that they came to America " to avoid oppression and cruel bondage; to shun persecution and designed ruin; to withdraw from the communion of idolaters; and to have an opportunity of worshipping God according to the dictates of conscience and the rules of His inspired Word." (6) Rutty's Weather and Seasons. (7) Bolton: Scotch-Irish Pioneers. (8) Ibid. (9) Letter of Archbishop King. Monck Mason xciii. Gordon: History of Ireland II. 212. Boulter to Newcastle, 1728. Letters I. 252. (10) King to Archbishop of Canterbury, 18th January, 1722-3. Commons Journals xvi., 387-418. (11) Reid: III. 224. (12) Rev. William Livingston. Woodrow's MS. Letters xxii., No. 109. (13) McSkimmin's Carrickfergus, 79-80. Gordon: II. 219. Burdy's Life of Skelton. (14) Gordon: II. 218. Burdy: 75. (15) Lecky: II. 47. (16) King's Letters. Mant: II. 331, 332. Lecky: I. 245. Gordon: II. 218. (17) Reid: III. 224. (18) Lecky: I. 245. (19) Lecky II. 47. (20) Froude: English in Ireland I. 140. (21) Hanna: The Scotch-Irish I. 74, 75, II. 6-13. For the general position see Mant: II. 98. Killen: II. 188, 189, 218, 219. Reid: III. 75. Lecky I. 112, 113. D'Alton: 298. (22) Bolton: Scotch-Irish Pioneers. (23) From Parker's List of Petitioners, as given in Witherow's

Appendix 59

Presbyterian Memorials, Second Series, pp. 5, 6, 7. Dr. J. B.
Woodburn has counted the names as given in Bolton, and
makes the total 320, of whom 11 signed with their marks.
(24) Smith: 261. (25) Parker: History of Londonderry, New
Hampshire: Letter of McGregor to Governor Shute. Perry:
The Scotch-Irish in New England. (26) Smith: 259. Perry.
(27) Smith: 260. (28) Parker: 137-139. (29) Speech of
General Steele at Peterborough Centennial Proceedings,
1839. Smith: 333. (30) Parker. Witherow: Presbyterian
Memorials: I. 241. (31) Parker: 137-139. (32) Perry: The
Scotch-Irish in New England. (33) Smith: 145, 150-9. (34)
Perry. (35) Perry. (36) Smith: 147. (37) Scarlet Letter, 12.
(38) Smith: 147-154. (39) Smith. Perry. (40) Carleton's
New Hampshire Worthies. Perry. Condon: The Irish Race
in America. Black: Scotland's Mark on America. (41)
Carleton. Perry. (42) Woodrow's MS. Letters, xx. 129.
(43) Life of King. 207. (44) Boulter's Letters, Oxford
Edition, 260, 261. (45) Ibid: 288. (46) Condon: 27. (47)
Whitelaw Reid: The Scot in America and the Ulster Scot,
31. (48) Lecky: I. 247. Killen: II. 261-2. (49) Hanna: II. 68.
(50) Reid: III. 226. Departmental Corr. (Dub. S.P. Office),
February 11th, 1728. Minutes of Tyrone Presbytery. (51)
Fiske: Old Virginia and Her Neighbours. II. 394. (52)
Lecky: II. 261. (53) Arthur Young: Tour in Ireland. (54)
Episodes from the Winning of the West, Chap. II. (55)
Second Scotch-Irish Congress: Proceedings, 175. (56) Kelley:
Scotch-Irish of Tennessee. Columbia, 1889. (57) Whitelaw
Reid: 33. (58) Dr. David Ramsay. (59) Governor Gilmer.
(60) John Dalzell: The Scotch-Irish in Western Pennsylvania
1890. (61) Whitelaw Reid: 42. (62) Black: 31. (63)
Campbell: The Scotch-Irish in Ohio. Condon. (64) Speech
at Springfield, Ohio. May 11th, 1893. (65) Temple: The
Scotch-Irish in East Tennessee. Bancroft. (66) Bancroft:
History of the United States V. 77. (67) Temple. Bancroft.
(68) Smith: 269. (69) Episodes from the Winning of the
West. (70) Custis: Personal Recollections. (71) Lecky: II.
261 (1878). Ramsay: History of the American Revolution
II. 218. McGee: History of the Irish Settlers in North

America. (72) History of the American Revolution, 597.
(73) Adolphus: History of England from the Accession of
George III. to the conclusion of peace in 1783. (74) Bryson:
The Scotch-Irish People. Alabama, 1890. (75) Historical
Review, I. 458. (76) Letter to Baron Steuben. (77) White-
law Reid: 41. Address of Colonel Colyar at Scotch-Irish
Congress, in Columbia, 1889. Condon. (78) Whitelaw Reid:
41. Bancroft. Condon. (79) Condon: 211. (80) Whitelaw
Reid: 20, 22. Black. (81) Armstrong: Life of Wayne. (82)
Lossing: Field Book of the Revolution. (83) Irving's Life of
Washington. Bancroft. (84) Condon. (85) Lossing. Condon.
(86) Condon. (87) Life of John Stark, by Caleb Stark. (88)
Lossing: Field Book. (89) Condon. (90) Lossing. (91)
Potter's American Monthly, May, 1876. (92) Smith: 147.
(93) Whitelaw Reid. (94) Condon. (95) Ibid. (96) Black.
(97) Black. Condon. (98) Robinson: The Prestons of
America. (99) Lossing. (100) Condon. (101) Bryson: The
Scotch-Irish People. Alabama, 1890. (102) Perry: The
Scotch-Irish in the North-East. Kelley: The Scotch-Irish in
Tennessee. Kelly: General Sam Houston, 1890. Black.
Life of General Shields. (103) Black: 63. (104) Colonel
William Fox: Statistics of the Civil War. Proceedings of
the Scotch-Irish Congress, Columbia, 1889, pp. 28-9. (105)
Whitelaw Reid. Condon. (106) Whitelaw Reid. Centennial
Number of Irish World, 1876. Lossing's Eminent Americans.
(107) Condon. Black. (108) Lossing's Eminent Americans.
Whitelaw Reid. Woodburn: The Ulster Scot. Henry: The
Scotch-Irish of the South. Letter of S. Randall to First
Scotch-Irish Congress, 1889. Black. Records of Orange
Court House, Virginia. (109) Whitelaw Reid: 50. Black: 4.
Lossing: Eminent Americans. MacDonald: Three Centuries
of American Democracy. Condon. (110) Webster: History
of the Presbyterian Church in America. Sprague's Annals
of the American Pulpit. Murphy: The Presbytery of the
Log College. (111) Hanna: II. 94. Webster. (112) Rev.
Samuel Blair. (113) The reference is to congregations in
Pennsylvania. (114) Sprague. (115) Ibid. (116) Ibid.
(117) Alexander: History of the Log College. Macloskie:

What the Scotch-Irish have done for Education, Columbia, 1889. (118) Sermon by Dr. James Steele at the Centennial Celebration of the First Reformed Presbyterian Church in New York, 1897. (119) Whitelaw Reid: 58. (120) Whitelaw Reid. Woodburn. Condon. Macloskie. (121) Letter of Benjamin Franklin from Paris, 1st July, 1784. The statement about the priests was made to Franklin by the Papal Nuncio in person, on the authority of a letter the Nuncio had received from Rome. Father Carroll was Superior or Prefect Apostolic for five years, till by direction of the Pope, the United States priests elected a bishop. Father Carroll's election was ratified in Rome in 1789, and he was consecrated in 1790. (122) Ibid. (123) Bishop England: Works III. 238 (124) Ibid. (125) 11th June, 1918. (126) Tour in Ireland II. 56. (127) History of New York, 133. (128) A Straight Deal, 246-7.

II

Names of some Ministers, Licentiates, Students, or Emigrants who went from Ulster and served in the Ministry of Presbyterian Churches in North America during the period 1680-1820, with the Presbytery of oversight, or district of origin where these have been ascertained, the date or approximate date of arrival, and the Provinces or States where they exercised their ministry.

" a " with date = before; Lic. = licentiate; Stud. = student; ord. = ordained; Pres. = President.

Alexander, David: Lic. Route P.; a. 1736; Pa.
Alison, Francis; Lic. Letterkenny P.; 1735; Pa.; Vice-Prov. Coll. of Phila.; D.D. Glas.
Alison, John, Lic.; a. 1756. Retd. to Ir.
Baird, Thomas Dickson; Gilford; 1802; S.C., Ohio, Pa.
Bay, Andrew; a. 1748; Pa., Md., L.I.

Beatty, Charles Clinton; Co. Antrim; 1729; Pa.; Chaplain Pa. troops, N,W. frontier.

Bertram, William; ord. Bangor P.; 1732; Pa.

Birch, T. L.; ord. in Ir.; 1801; W.Pa.

Black, John; Co. Antrim; 1797; W.Pa.; Pres. Duquesne Coll.; D.D.

Black, Samuel; Lic. Armagh P.; a. 1735; Pa., Va., N.C.

Blackstock, William; Lic. Down P. (Burgher); a. 1794: N.C., S.C.

Blair, John; a. 1733; Pa., N.Y.; Vice-Pres. Princetown Coll.

Blair, Samuel; a. 1730; N.J., Pa.; Principal New London Academy.

Bothwell, David; Lic. Monaghan P.; 1789; Ga.

Boyce, John; a. 1783; S.C.

Boyd, Adam; Lic. Coleraine P.; 1723; Pa.

Boyd, Alexander; Stud.; 1748; Me., Pa.

Boyd, James; a. 1769; Pa.

Boyd, William; Min. Macosquin; 1718, with petition to Gov. Shute; retd. to Ir.; inst. Taboyne, 1725.

Bratton, Thomas; 1711; Md.

Brown, John; a. 1749; Va., Ky.

Brown, John; Co. Antrim; a. 1779; S.C., Ga.; Prof. Univ. S.C.; Pres. Univ. Ga.; D.D. Coll. N.J.; soldier in the war 1679-81.

Cannon, John; 1788; S.C.

Campbell, Alexander; 1809; W.Va., Tenn., Ky.; with his father, Rev. Thomas C. founded the Baptist Ch. "Disciples of Christ."

Campbell, Thomas; Lic. Markethill P.; 1807; W.Pa., Va., Tenn., Ky.

Campbell, Benjamin; Ballykelly; 1729; Md.

Campbell, Joseph; Omagh; 1797; N.J.; D.D. Lafayette Coll.

Campbell, Charles; Min. Dunboe; 1801; Pa.

Carlisle, Hugh; Lic. Monaghan P.; 1735; Pa., N.J.

Cathcart, Robert; Lic.; 1730; Pa.

Cathcart, Robert; Lic. Route P.; 1790; Pa.; D.D. Queen's Coll., N.J.

Cavin, Samuel; Lic.; 1737; Pa., Va.

Clark, Matthew; Min. Boveedy; 1728; N.H.; soldier in Derry during the siege.

Clark, Thomas; Min. Cahans; 1764; N.Y., N.C.; Diploma in Medicine, Glas.

Conn, Hugh; Magilligan; a. 1715; Md.

Cooper, Robert; 1741; Pa.; D.D. Dickinson Coll.

Cornwall, William; Min. Clogher; 1718; Me.

Craig, John; Donegore; 1734; W.Va.

Craig, John, Min. Coronery; 1793; Pa.

Creaghead, Thomas; Lic. Strabane P.; 1714; Mass., Pa.

Cross, Robert; Lic. Derry P.; 1717; Pa., L.I., Phila.

Cummings, Charles; a. 1767; Va.; frontier ch., with minister and people always armed at service.

Davis, Samuel; a. 1692; Del.; member of first Presby.

Dobbin, Alexander; Derry; 1772; Pa.

Donnelly, Thomas; Co. Donegal; 1791; S.C.

Dorrance, Samuel; Lic. Coleraine P.; 1719; Conn.

Dunlop, Robert; Co. Antrim; 1736; Me.

Dunlop, Samuel; Lic. Coleraine P.; 1737; N.H.

Elder, John; Lic. Coleraine P.; a. 1738; capt. of Rangers, with command of block-houses on the frontier.

Elliott, William; ord. Armagh P.; 1718.

Finley, James; Co. Armagh; 1734; Md., Pa.

Finley, Samuel; Co. Armagh; 1734; Md.; Pres., Coll. of N.J.; D.D. Glas.

Fisher, Hugh; ord. Armagh P.; 1715; S.C.

Fitzgerald, Edward; 1718; Mass.

Gelston, Samuel; Lic.; 1715; L.I., Pa.

Gibson, William; Min. Kellswater; 1797; Vt., Pa., N.J.

Gibson, Robert; Ballymena; 1797; Pa., N.Y.

Glasgow, Patrick; a. 1736; Md.

Glendy, John; Min. Maghera; 1799; Baltimore; Chaplain, Senate and House of Reps.; D.D. Univ. of Md.

Goudy, Alexander; Min. Donaghadee; 1792.

Gray, James, Lic. Monaghan P.; 1797; N.Y., Phila.

Hampton, John; ord. in Ulster; 1705; Md.; member of the first Presbytery.

Harper, James; Min. Knockloughrim; 1798; Va.

Hemphill, John; a. 1792; N.J.; D.D. Dickinson Coll.

Hemphill, Samuel; Lic. Strabane P.; 1734; Phila.

Henry, John; ord. Dublin P.; 1709; Md., Va.

Henry, George; Min. of Narrow-water; 1764.

Heron, Robert; Lic. Armagh P.; 1735; Va.

Hidelston, John; ord. Belfast P.; 1784; credentials to Newcastle P. 1785.

Hillhouse, James; ord. Derry P.; 1719; Conn.

Holmès, William; ord. Strabane P.; 1714; Mass.

Hook, Henry; ord. Dublin P.; a. 1718; N.J., Del.

Houston, Joseph; Lic.; 1724; Md., N.Y.

Hull, James Foster; Lic. Bangor P.; 1798; Ga., New Orleans; Episcopal orders, 1814.

Hunter, Humphrey; Derry; 1759; N.C.; soldier in the war.

Jameson, Robert; ord. Templepatrick P.; 1734; Del.

Jarvie, John; ord. Belfast P.; 1715; S.C.

Johnson, John; Lic. Belfast P.; 1786.

Johnston, William; Co. Tyrone; 1736; N.H., N.Y.

Kennedy, James; Lic.; a. 1796; Tenn.

Kennedy, Samuel; Lic. Dromore P.; 1772; S.C.

Kennedy, Thomas; Lic. Bangor P.; a. 1771; S.C.

Kerr, Joseph; Stud.; Co. Derry; 1801; W.Pa., Ohio; D.D.

King, William; 1792; S.C.

Kinkead, John; a. 1753; Pa., N.H.

Kirkpatrick, Robert; Min. Portglenone; a. 1773.

Knox, Hugh; 1751; Isl. of Saba, Isl. of St. Croix; D.D. Glas.

Knox, William; Lic. Route P.; 1767; S.C.

Laing, Robert; Lic. Down P.; 1722; Md.

Latta, James; 1738; Pa.; soldier in the war, and chaplain also; D.D. Univ. of Pa.

Legat, —; Divinity Stud.; credentials to Newcastle P. 1733.

Lindsay, Colin; Min. Dundalk; a. 1790.

Logue, John; Min. Buckna; 1772; N.J., Pa.

Appendix   65

Lynd, Matthew; Min. Limavady; 1774; W.Pa.

McAuley, William; Min. Tullyallen; 1794; N.Y.; frontier minister.

McClenachan, William; a. 1734; Me., Mass., Va., Phila.; Episcopal orders, 1754.

McClintock, Robert; ord. Bangor P. 1775; 1772; again in 1781; S.C.

McConnell, James; Lic. Route P.; 1797; Pa.

McCook, Archibald; Stud.; credentials to Newcastle P. 1726; Del.

McCosh, John; a. 1785; W.Va.

McCrea, James; a. 1737; N.J.

McDowall, Alexander; 1737; Md.; Principal, N. London Acad.

McDowell, Alexander B.; a. 1753; Mass.

McGarragh, James; ord. at Bready for Amer.; 1791; S.C.

McGill, Hugh; Min. Clenanees; 1772; Pa.

McGregore, James, Min. Aghadowey; 1718; N.H.; soldier in siege of Derry.

McGregore, David; 1718; N.H.

McHenry, Francis; Lic. Monaghan P.; 1738; Pa. (Born Rathlin Isl.)

McKee, David; ord. Bangor P.; 1768; S.C.

McKee, William; 1784; credentials to Synod, 1785.

McKennan, William; a. 1752; Del.

McKinley, Henry; Min. Moville; 1771; W.Pa.; soldier for a time in the war.

McKinney, James; 1793; reconstituted the Ref. Presby., Phila., 1798.

McKinstry, John; 1719.

McKnight, Charles; Stud.; 1740; N.J.; imprisoned by the British.

McLin, Robert; a. 1785; S.C.

McMaster, Gilbert; 1791; N.Y., Ind.; D.D.

McMullan, Alexander; Min. Broughshane; 1773; S.C.

McMullen, Peter; Min. Ahoghill; 1789; S.C.

McWhirr, William; ord. Killyleagh P.; 1783; Va., Ga.; D.D. Frankil Coll.

McWhorter, Alexander; Stud.; 1730; died before completing his studies for the ministry.

Mackie, Josias; a. 1692; Va.

Madden, Campbell; Lic.; 1820; S.C.

Madowell, John; Lic. Killyleagh P.; 1736; Phila.

Mairs, George; Min. Cootehill; 1793; N.Y.

Mairs, James; Lic. Monaghan P.; 1793; N.Y.

Makemie, Francis; Lic. Laggan P.; 1682; Barbadoes, Va., Md., S.C.; member of the first Presbytery; "Father of American Presbyterian Church."

Malcomson, James; Lic. Belfast P.; 1792; S.C.

Marshall, Robert; Co. Down; a. 1790; Ky.

Martin, James; ord. Templepatrick P.; 1734; Del.

Martin, James; Min. Bangor; 1775; Pa.

Martin, William; Min. Vow; a. 1775; church burned and himself imprisoned by British forces.

Miles, John; Lic. Bangor P.; 1798.

Miller, Alexander; Min. Ardstraw; 1753; Va.

Miller, Robert; a. 1755; S.C.

Moor, Solomon; Newtownards; a. 1768; N.H.

Moorhead, John; Newtownards; 1727; Boston.

Morrison, Hugh; Lic. Letterkenny P.; 1788; Mass.

Murray, John; 1762; Phila., Me.

Orr, Robert; Lic.; 1715; N.J.

Orr, William; Stud.; 1730; Md.; Episcopal orders, 1736.

Patterson, Joseph; Co. Down; 1773; W.Pa.; soldier in the war.

Paul, John; Lic. Route P.; a. 1736; Md.

Porter, Samuel; 1783; W.Pa.

Potts, George; Lic. Monaghan P.; 1797; Phila.

Pringle, Francis; Min. Gilnahirk; 1799; Pa.

Ralston, Samuel; Co. Donegal; 1794; Pa.; D.D. Washington Coll.

Rea, William; Min. Dundonald; 1765; Tenn.

Reagh, Joseph; Min. Fahan; 1769.

Appendix 67

Reilly, John; 1797; S.C.

Renwick, John; ord. for Amer.; 1770; S.C.

Riddell, John; Min. Donacloney; 1794; W.Va.; D.D. Washington Coll.

Roan, John; a. 1736; Va., Pa.

Rogers, James; Co. Monaghan; 1789; S.C.

Ronaldson, William; Min. Loughaghery; 1773; S.C.

Rosburgh, John; 1735; Pa.; soldier in the war, and also chaplain; murdered by Hessians.

Rutherford, Robert; 1729; Vt.

Sanckey, Richard; a. 1735; Va.

Sloss, James Long; Bellaghy; 1803; Ala.

Smith, Robert; Londonderry; 1730; Pa.; D.D. Coll. of N.J.; Mod. of Second General Assembly.

Smith, Sampson; a. 1750; Va., Pa.

Smith, Thomas; Min. Randalstown; 1799; Pa.

Steel, John; Lic. Londonderry P.; a. 1744; Pa.; commanded Pa. troops in the French war.

Steel, Robert; a. 1810; Pa.; D.D. Jefferson Coll.

Stevenson, Hugh; Stud.; a. 1726; Md., Phila.

Sturgeon, Robert; Lic. Coleraine P.; a. 1726; Me., N.Y.

Tate, Joseph; a. 1748; Md.

Tennent, William; ord. by Bishop of Down; 1718; recd. into Pres. Ch. by Phila. Synod; N.Y., Pa.; founded the Log College, which was the beginning of Princeton.

Tennent, Gilbert; Co. Armagh; 1718; N.J.; Phila.

Tennent, William; Co. Armagh; 1718; N.J.

Tennent, John; Co. Armagh; 1718; N.J.

Tennent, Charles; Coleraine; 1718; Del., Md.

Thompson, —; Lic. Tyrone P.; a. 1734; recd. by N. England Presbytery

Thomson, John; Lic.; 1715; Del., Pa., W.Va., N.C.

Thomson, Samuel; Lic. Coleraine P.; 1737; Pa., Md.

Trail, William; Min. Lifford; fined and imprisoned because of Fast apptd. by Laggan P.; 1684; Md.

Weddel, James; Newry; a. 1745; Va.; D.D. Dickinson Coll.

Walker, James; Lic. Down P.; 1799; Pa.

Walkinshaw, Hugh; Co. Antrim; 1819; W.Pa.

Wallace, Robert; Co. Armagh; 1811; W.Pa., Ohio.
Warden, David Bailie; Lic. Bangor P.; 1799.
Warnock, Samuel;
Warwick, Robert; ord. for Amer.; 1792; Pa., Ohio.
Watt, James; Boardmills; a. 1794; Pa.
Wilson, John; 17th century; Conn., Md.
Wilson, John; Min. Carlingford and Dundalk; 1729; Pa.,
Boston.
Wilson, John; 1729; N.H.
Wilson, Thomas; Min. Killybegs and Inver; 1681; Md.
Woodside, James; min. Garvagh and Dunboe; 1718; Me.
Wylie, Samuel B.; Ballymena, 1797; Phila.; Vice-Prov.
Univ. of Pa.; D.D.
Young, Samuel; Min. Magherally; 1718; Del.

III

Names of some American-born ministers of the period
1730-1820, whose parents were from Ulster. The dates are
of licensure, unless otherwise stated. It is to be understood
that only a small number of such ministers are to be
found in this list. Contractions as in II.

Allison, Patrick; 1763; Baltimore; D.D. Univ. of Pa.
Baird, Samuel; son of Rev. Thomas Dickson Baird. (App. II.)
Baird, Ebenezer;   do.
Baird, James;   do.
Blair, Samuel; 1764; Boston; Phila.; Chaplain to Congress;
D.D. Univ. of Pa.; son of Rev. Samuel Blair. (App. II.)
Blair, John D.; 1785; Va.; son of Rev. John Blair. (App. II.)
Boyd, Adam; a. 1776; N.C.; army chaplain.
Boyd, William; 1783; N.J.
Caldwell, David; 1763; N.C.

Appendix

Caldwell, James; 1760; N.J.; Chaplain to the Jersey Brigade; wife shot, church burned, and a price on his head. Supplied troops with hymn-books for bullet wadding in the attack on Springfield. Commissary-General at Chatham. Shot by a militia-man. Monument over his grave by Cincinnati of N.J. John C. Calhoun was his great-grandson.

Cannon, James S.; 1796; N.J.; D.D.

Creaghead, Alexander; 1734; Md., Va., N.C.; believed to be son of Rev. Thomas Creaghead. (App. II.).

Cummins, Francis; 1780; S.C., Ga.; present at the reading of the Mecklenburg Decl.; served in the army, and in several battles; Member of S.C. Convention; teacher, and Andrew Jackson a pupil; active missionary, and about 20 congns. considered him their minister; D.D. Univ. of Ga.

Duffield, George; 1756; W.Pa., Phila.; frontier min. for a time, and army chaplain with a price on his head; John Adams a member of his church in Phila.; first stated Clerk of the General Assembly; D.D. Yale.

Doak, Samuel; 1777; Va.; frontier minister for a time; Pres. Washington Coll.; D.D. Washington Coll.; D.D. Greenville Coll.

Finley, John Evans; Missionary in Kentucky from 1795; son of Rev. James Finley. (App. II.).

Grier, Nathan; 1786; Pa.

Grier, James; 1775; Pa.

Graham, William; 1775; founded Liberty Hall, which became Washington Coll.; captain of volunteers.

Graham, Samuel L.; 1818; frontier missionary, Va. and Ind.; min. in Va.; Prof. Union Theol. Sem.; D.D. Union Coll., N.Y.

Hall, James; 1775; Mass.; commanded a troop of cavalry on a campaign in N.C.; offered commission as Brig.-Gen.; D.D. Princeton; D.D. Univ. of N.C.

Hamill, Samuel, D.D.; son of Robert Hamill, who emigrated from Ulster to Pa., late 18th cent.

Hamill, Hugh, D.D.;   do.

Inglis, James; 1801; Baltimore; D.D. Coll. of N.J.

Johnston, John; 1806; Md.; D.D. Lafayette Coll.

King, John; 1767; Pa.; D.D. Dickinson Coll.; 4th Mod. of General Assembly.

Kirkpatrick, John L.; 1814; W.Va.; served in the army in the war.

Latta, Francis Alison; ord. 1796; Del., Pa., son of Dr. James Latta. (App. II.).

Latta, William; grad. 1794; Pa.; D.D. Lafayette Coll.; son of Dr. James Latta.

Latta, John Ewing; ord. 1800; Del.; Permanent Clerk of General Assembly; son of Dr. James Latta.

Lynd, John; 1807; Pa.; son of Matthew (App. II.).

Matthews, John; 1801; N.C., Va.; Prof. Hanover Coll., Ind.; D.D. Washington Coll.

Mitchell, James; 1781; Ky.

Marques, Thomas; 1793; W.Pa.; frontier minister with log church in the woods.

Martin, Samuel; 1793; Pa., Md.; D.D. Jefferson Coll.

McAden, Hugh; 1755; N.C.

McChord, James; 1809; Pres. Bourboin.

McJimsey, John; 1794; N.Y.; D.D.

McMillan, John; a. 1776; Pa.; Founder of. Jefferson Coll.; D.D.

McMurray, William; 1809; N.Y.; D.D.

McWhorter, Alexander; 1758; N.J., N.C., Pa.; army chaplain; Pres. Charlotte Coll., N.C.; D.D. Yale.

McRee, James; 1778; N.C.; D.D. Univ. of N.C.

Patterson, Robert; ord. C. 1796 near Pittsburg; son of Rev. Joseph Patterson. (App. II.).

Patterson, James; 1808; N.J., Phila.

Power, James; 1772; W.Pa.; D.D. Jefferson Coll.

Porter, Samuel; ord. 1811; Md.; son of Rev. Samuel Porter (App. II.).

Potts, George; Min. of Univ. Place Church, N.Y. city; D.D.; son of Rev. George Charles Potts (App. II.).

Ramsey, William; ord. 1756; Conn.

Rodgers, John; 1747; Pa.; Del., N.J., N.Y.; Chaplain to
Heath's Brigade; Chaplain to the Convention of N.Y.
State; Vice-Chancellor Univ. of N.Y.; Mod. of the first
General Assembly; D.D. Edin.

Read, Thomas; 1768; Del.; soldier in the war; guide to
Washington in retreat from Stanton; D.D. Coll. of N.J.

Scott, George McIlroy; father came from Ulster in 1741.
Missionary to Indians in Ohio; one of the founders of
Washington Coll.; D.D.

Smith, William R.; 1776; Del., N.J.; son of Dr. Robert
Smith. (App. II.).

Smith, Samuel Stanhope; 1773; Pres. Coll. of N.J.; D.D.
Yale; LL.D. Harvard; son of Dr. Robert Smith.

Smith, John Blair; 1777; Va., Phila.; Pres. Hampden Sidney
Coll.; first Pres. Union Coll., N.Y.; captain of
Volunteers and served in the war; D.D. Coll. of N.J.;
son of Dr. Robert Smith.

Steele, John; 1797; Ohio.

Stephenson, James White; 1789; S.C. Tenn.; enlisted and
served throughout the war; D.D. Univ. of S.C.

Taggart, Samuel; 1776; Mass.; Member of U.S. Congress.

Tate, Matthew; a. 1789; S.C.; son of Joseph (II.).

Tennent, William Mackay; ord. 1772; Conn., Pa.; D.D. Yale;
son of Rev. Charles Tennent. (App. II.).

Tennent, William; 1762; Conn., S.C.; Member of Prov.
Cong. of S.C.; son of Rev. William Tennent, jun.
(App. II.).

Waddell, Moses; 1792; Ga.; Pres. Univ. of Ga.; D.D.
Columbia Coll.

Wilson, Matthew; 1754; Del.; D.D. Univ. of Pa.; doctor
also, with a large medical practice.

Wilson, Robert G.; 1793; S.C., Ohio; Pres. Univ. of Ohio;
D.D. Coll. of N.J.

IV

Names of some American-born ministers of the period
1752-1820, of Ulster extraction, but not of parents from
Ulster. Those marked with an asterick had grand-parents
from Ulster. As in the case of III., this list is merely
fragmentary. Contractions as in II.

*Alexander, Archibald, D.D.; 1791; Ky., Phila.; Pres. Hampden Sidney Coll.; Prof. Princeton; Mod. Gen. Ass.

*Anderson, John, D.D.; 1791; N.C., S.C., Ky., Tenn., Pa.

Anderson, Isaac; 1802; Tenn.

Armstrong, James F.; 1777; N.Y., N.J.; Chaplain to 2nd Brigade, Md. troops in the war.

*Armstrong, Amzi, D.D.; 1795; N.J.; Pres. Bloomfield Coll.

Armstrong, William J.; 1818; N.J., Va.; D.D.

Baxter, George A., D.D.; 1797; Pres. Washington Coll., Va.; Prof. of Theology, Union Coll.

*Brown, Matthew, D.D., LL.D.; 1799; Pa.; First Pres. Washington Coll., Pa.; Pres. Jefferson Coll., Pa.

Blackburn, Gideon, D.D.; 1792; Tenn., Ky.; frontier min. and Indian missionary; Pres. Centre Coll., Ky.

*Caldwell, Samuel; a. 1792; N.C.

*Chamberlain, Jeremiah; 1817; Pa., Ky.; Pres. Central Coll.; D.D.

*Doak, John Whitefield; 1809; Va., Pres. Washington Coll.; M.D.

*Doak, Samuel; bro. of above; Pres. Bethel Coll.; D.D.

Dickey, Ebenezer, D.D.; 1794; Pa.

Dickey, John McE.; 1814; Ind.

*Duncan, John; 1811; Baltimore; D.D.

Ewing, John, D.D.; 1758; Phila.; visited England, and recd. the freedom of the cities of Glasgow, Montrose, Dundee, and Perth; had several interviews with the Prime Minister, Lord North.

*Finley, Robert; a. 1795; Pres. Univ. of Ga.

Gallagher, James; 1815; Tenn.; Pres. Marion Coll.

*Glass, Joseph; a. 1820; Va.
*Grier, John F., D.D.; 1810; Pa.
Grier, Isaac; 1791; Pa.
*Gilliland, James; 1794; S.C., Ohio.
Irwin, Nathaniel; 1772; Pa.; Mod. of General Assembly.
Linn, John Blair, D.D.; 1798; Phila.
*Linn, William; 1775; Md., N.J., N.Y.; army chaplain; D.D.
*Lyle, John; 1797; Va., Ky.
*Macurdy, Elisha; 1799; Ohio.
*McDowell, William A., D.D.; 1813; N.J., S.C.; Mod. Gen. Assembly.
*McDowell, John, D.D.; brother of above.
*McPheeters, William, D.D.; 1802; Ky., Ohio, N.C.
McCready, James; 1788; Va., N.C., Ky., Ohio.
Rankin, Adam; 1752; Ky.
Ramsey, Samuel G.; 1795; Ky.
*Reid, William S., D.D.; 1806; Va.; Pres. Hampden Sidney Coll.
*Scott, John W.; son of George McEll. Scott (III.); father of Mrs. Benjamin Harrison; D.D.
*Smith, W. R.; 1820; Pa.
Wharey, James; 1818; N.C., Va.
*Wilson, James P., D.D.; 1804; Del., Phila.
Willson, James R.; 1807; Pa., N.J.; D.D.
*Williams, Joshua, D.D.; 1797; Pa.

V

Some names of ministers from Ireland or of Irish origin in the Protestant Episcopal Church in N. America, in the early period. Dates are of arrival in America, unless otherwise stated. Contractions as in II.

Johnstone, Gideon; 1707; S.C.
Henderson, Jacob; 1710; Del., Md.
Jenny, Robert; 1715; N.Y., L.I., Phila.; LL.D.

McSparran, James; Dungiven; 1721; R.I.; D.D.
Cummings, Archibald; 1726; Phila.
Berkeley, George; 1728; R.I.; D.D.; Bish. of Cloyne.
Browne, Arthur; 1729; R.I., N.H.
Browne, Marmaduke; son of above; R.I., N.H.
Orr, William; ord. 1736; S.C.
Thomson, William; 1750; Pa.
Glasgow, Patrick; 1753; Md
McClenachan, William; 1754; Va., Phila.
Barton, Thomas; 1755; Pa.
Inglis, Charles; a. 1759; Del., N.Y.; D.D.; Bish. of Nova Scotia.
Bowden, John; a. 1770; N.Y., L.I., St. Croix, Conn.; D.D.
Andrews, William; a. 1770; N.Y., Va.; Bish. of N.C. but not consecrated.
Petticrew, Charles; ord. 1775; N.C.
Tate, Matthew; a. 1789; S.C.
Barry, Edmund; 1799; N.Y., Md.; D.D.
Hull, James; ord. 1814; Ga.
Ogilby, John; 1815; N.Y.; D.D.
McElhinney, George; a. 1816; Baltimore, Md.; D.D.
Patterson, Stephen; 1821; Miss.
Presstman, Stephen; ord. 1822; Va., Del.
Wylie, Andrew; ord. 1841; D.D.; Pres. Jefferson Coll.; Pres. Indiana Coll.
Dunlop, George Kelly; Sixmilecross; Bish. of Arizona.

VI

ULSTERMEN IN EDUCATION

The part played was outstanding. William Tennent founded the Log College at Neshaminy, Pa., in 1727. His pupil, Samuel Blair, started a classical academy at Fagg's Manor, Pa., in 1740. Another pupil, Samuel Finley, founded Nottingham Academy, Pa., in 1744. Blair's pupil, Robert

Smith, opened Pequea Academy, Pa., about 1751. These were the four most famous classical schools in that region during that period, and very many distinguished Americans were pupils of Tennent, Blair, Finley and Smtih. It is now regarded as an unquestioned fact that the beginning of the great Princeton University was the Log College of Tennent.

Robert Smith's pupil, John McMillan, founded a school which was the nucleus of Jefferson College. Another pupil, Samuel Martin, had a school in York Co., Pa., near the close of the century. There were also the schools of Dodd at Redstone in S.W.Pa., of Blair at Newville, and of King at Canococheague. These Western academies developed into Washington and Jefferson College.

In N.C. was the school of David Caldwell, called the Eton of the South; in Va., the academy of James W. Stephenson, and the seminary of Samuel Smith, which became Hampden Sidney College. The South had also Anderson's academy at Maryville. Samuel Doak founded the first classical school in the Mississippi Valley, at Salem, in 1780. It was chartered as Martin Academy, and became Washington College in 1795. Doak also founded Tusculum College at Greenville, which was later united with Greenville College. Samuel Carrick founded Blount College in 1794, which is now the University of Tenn. Davidson Academy, Nashville, became Davidson College, and Thomas Craighead was its first President.

There is enough to shew the quality of the Ulster achievement in Education, collegiate and university, and it is not necessary to carry the statement further. The work was chiefly pioneer, and the number of classical and elementary schools founded by our people is legion. A few names, however, may be added, of Ulster interest, which may help to reveal still further our prominence in the collegiate life of the time. The dates are dates of birth, and, for the most part, only College Presidents are included.

Allison, Francis; 1705; Vice-Pres. Coll. of Phila.

Finley, Samuel; 1715; Pres. of Princeton.

Blair, John; 1720; Vice-Pres. Princeton.

Rodgers, John; 1727; Vice-Chanc. Univ. of N.Y.

Patterson, Robert; 1743; Vice-Prov. Univ. of Pa. (His son Robert was also Vice-Prov.).

Graham, William; 1745; Pres. Washington Coll. (Now Washington and Lee Univ.).

Smith, Samuel S.; 1750; Pres. of Princeton.

Craighead, Thomas; 1750; Pres. Davidson Coll. (Now the Univ. of Nashville).

McMillan, John; 1752; Founder of Jefferson Coll., Pa.

Smith, John B.; 1756; Pres. Hampden Sidney Coll.; Pres. Union Coll., Schenectady, N.Y.

McKeen, Joseph; 1757; Pres. Bowdoin Coll.

Brown, John; 1763; Pres. Univ. of Ga.

Wilson, Robert G.; 1768; Pres. Univ. of Ohio.

Black, John; 1768; Pres. Duquesne Coll., Ky.

Waddell, Moses; 1770; Pres. Univ. of Ga.

Baxter, George; 1771; Pres. Washington Coll., Va.

Finley, Robert; 1772; Pres. Univ. of Ga.

Alexander, Arch.; 1772; Pres. Hampden Sidney Coll.

Blackburn, Gideon; 1772; Pres. Centre Coll., Ky.

Caldwell, Joseph; 1773; Pres. Univ. of N.C.

Wylie, Samuel B.; 1773; Vice-Prov. Univ. of Pa.

Brown, Matthew; 1776; Pres. Jefferson Coll., Pa.; Pres. Washington Coll., Pa.

Doak, Samuel; 1777; Pres. Washington Coll., Va.

Doak, John W.; succeeded his father in 1818 as Pres. Washington Coll.

Reid, William S.; 1778; Pres. Hampden Sidney Coll., Va.

Gallagher, James; 1792; Pres. Marion Coll., Ohio.

Chamberlain, Jeremiah; 1794; Pres. Centre Coll., Ky.; Pres. Jackson Coll., La.

Rollins, James S.; 1812; " Pater Universitatis Missouri-eusis."

VIII

SOME PROVINCIAL OR STATE GOVERNORS OF
ULSTER BIRTH OR EXTRACTION

The dates are of birth

James Logan; 1674; Pa.
John McKinly; 1721; Del.
John Hancock; 1737; Mass.
Thomas Nelson; 1738; Va.
George Clinton; 1739; N.Y.
John Rutledge; 1739; S.C.
Edward Rutledge; 1749; S.C.
Jeremiah Smith; 1759; N.H.
John Bell; 1765; N.H.
Samuel Dinsmoor; 1766; N.H.
William Findlay; 1768; Pa.
De Witt Clinton; 1769; N.Y.
Jeremiah Morrow; 1770; Ohio.
Samuel Bell; 1770; N.H.
James Miller; 1776; Ark.
Joseph Read; 1778; Pa.
Andrew Pickens; 1779; S.C.
Allen Trimble; 1783; Ohio.
Patrick Noble; 1787; S.C.
Charles Polk; 1788; Del.
Joseph M. Harper; 1789; N.H.
William Patterson; 1790; N.J.
Robert P. Dunlap; 1794; Me.
William L. Ewing; 1795; Ill.
John M. Patton; 1797; Va.
Samuel Dinsmoor; 1799; N.H.
Thomas McKean; 1799; Pa.
Hugh J. Anderson; 1801; Me.
Noah Martin; 1801; N.H.
Robert M. Patton; 1809; Ala.
John B. Cochran; 1809; Del.
Samuel W. Black; c. 1815; Neb.

Peter H. Bell; 1812; Tex.

James W. Grimes; 1816; Iowa.

John W. Geary; 1819; Pa.

William E. Stevenson; 1820; W.Va.

Charles H. Bell; 1823; N.H.

VIII

A FEW AMERICAN NAMES OF ULSTER INTEREST FROM THE EARLY PERIOD

Dates are dates of birth

William Killen; 1722; First Chief Justice of Del.

James Adams; c. 1732; Founded the "Wilmington Courant" in 1762.

Adam Boyd; 1738; Issued the first number of the "Cape Fear Mercury" in 1769.

John Rutledge; 1739; Chief Justice of the U.S. Supreme Court.

Andrew Brown; 1744; Published the first issue of the "Philadelphia Gazette."

John Dunlap; 1747; First printed the Declaration of Independence.

David Ramsey; 1749; Eminent historian: "History of South Carolina."

Robert Dinsmoor; 1757; American poet.

Robert Fulton; 1765; Pioneer steam-boat builder.

Hugh McCall; 1767; Historian: "History of Georgia."

Andrew Jackson; 1767; Justice of the Supreme Court of Tenn.

John B. Gibson; 1780; Chief Justice of the Supreme Court of Pa.

John C. Calhoun; 1782; Vice-Pres.; Sec. of War; Sec. of State.

Alexander Porter; c. 1785; Justice of the Supreme Court of Louisiana.

Appendix

William Patterson; 1790; Associate Justice of the U.S. Supreme Court.

Samuel Nelson; 1792; Associate Justice of the U.S. Supreme Court.

Thomas McKean; 1799; Chief Justice of the Supreme Court of Pa.

William W. Campbell; 1806; Eminent historian and jurist.

William Orr; 1808; First to make and sell paper containing wood fibre.

Cyrus McCormick; 1809; Inventor of the reaping machine.

Edgar Allan Poe; 1809; Poet and writer.

James McKim; 1810; Founder of the "New York Nation."

Asa Gray; 1810; Famous American botanist.

Horace Greeley; 1811; Founder of the "New York Tribune"; Presidential candidate; Anti-slavery leader.

William V. McKean; 1820; Editor-in-Chief of the "Philadelphia Public Ledger."

John C. Breckenridge; 1821; Vice-Pres.; Major-Gen.; Confederate Sec. of War.

Joseph Medill; 1823; Proprietor of the "Chicago Tribune."

Robert Bonner; 1824; Founder of the "New York Ledger."

Grier, Robert; son of Isaac Grier (IV.); Justice of the U.S. Supreme Court.

Morse, Samuel Finley B.; 1791; inventor of the electro-magnetic telegraph; Finley, from his great-grandfather, Samuel Finley (II).